Opposite is a drawing of the wrought iron latch and door of the barn which stood for so many years near Shelving Rock Falls. The old structure with its adz hewn beams and whittled oaken pegging has been torn down. Yet the memory of such a sturdy construction remains part of precious American heritage here as elsewhere.

Elsa Kny Steinback

SWEET PEAS

AND A WHITE BRIDGE

On Lake George When Steam Was King

Illustrations by the Author

SWEET PEAS AND A WHITE BRIDGE

Library of Congress Catalog Card Number
74-26238
ISBN 0-932052-22-3

Printed in the United States of America

North Country Books, Inc.
311 Turner Street
Utica, New York 13502

For two people on a white bridge, for Jane, Billie and Addie, and a little mountain called Shelving Rock.

"The workmanship of souls is by those inaudible words of the earth . . .

The earth does not withhold, it is generous enough
The truths of the earth continually wait, they are not so conceal'd either."

Walt Whitman

Introduction

Lake George has witnessed its share of this nation's history in the making. The region didn't simply become known through a slow westward infiltration of settlers in search of greener pastures, unexploited natural resources. This was to come later. The lake was part of a great strategic waterway. It saw the pageantry and the horrors of the colonial wars out of which came America. During those often savage conflicts of the 18 century the lake's mountains echoed back the alien skirl of High-landers' bagpipes, the martial music of fife and drum along with the blood chilling warwhoop it had long known. It saw savage tortures inflicted, heard the screams of the victims. In gentler vein the lake must often have heard songs of lands across the sea sung by homesick voices. The waters reflected brilliant uniforms flashing with gold epaulettes and braid, men in coonskin caps and fringed deerskin or the butternut dyed homespun of Yankee Doodle Dandy. The lake was well acquainted with scalplocks laced with eagle feathers above faces that seemed hardly human under ghastly warpaint! With it all the lake discovered long ago that the blood of all races and creeds runs the same red.

The future nation's destiny indeed sometimes hung in the balance on Lakes George and Champlain. The pages which follow deal little with those wartime days for their story has been told down through the years often and well. Rather have I tried to paint a sort of genre picture of days when the wars were done, when the lumber industry became king for many years, when the great age of steam brought immeasurable changes to the land everywhere. Due largely to the latter the lake's beauty became world famous and resort business gradually superseded lumber-ing along the shores. The book tells of early settlers and later ones, of steamboatmen and passengers, of hotelmen and their guests and employees, all in the age to which good Queen Victoria gave her name. The story is brought almost up to the present so it's bound to set some to remembering while others may find interest in learning how life was lived along the lake not so very long ago. The later chapters deal specifically with the lovely area known as the lake's narrows.

During the 19th century as the Adirondack Mountains became more and more popular with vacationers and sportsmen local personages emerged who became famous far and wide. These were the Adirondack guides. Not the least known was Orson Phelps better remembered as "Old Mountain Phelps." This gentleman had, furthermore, an approach to the language which is part of mountain lore today.

Phelps would ask prospective clients whether they preferred "a reg'lar walk or a random scoot?" The differentiation is obvious. It occurred to me that this book has followed both ways. It relates historical fact but sometimes wanders off into tales quite outside the mainstream of history.

It was also Phelps who coined a description of his personal Nirvana which was the summit of Mt. Marcy, highest of the Adirondack high peaks. It was his most beloved mountain. (He spoke of it as "Mt. Mercy."). On its summit he said he felt what he called "heaven up-h'isted-ness". Most of us have met this feeling, unexpectedly and in unplanned moments. It is an essence found in unspoiled wilderness places to a high degree. It has requirements for it lies in great semi-intangibles which demand seeing eyes, atuned ears and the need to comprehend what one sees, hears, feels and perhaps consequently what one is.

The essence can be found along this lovely lake. It can rise from ephemeral things, from the song tall pines sing in a wind, from the stunning impact of white birch against rain-dark forest, from the scent of cedar which is like no other scent. These are the trees which spread ballerina skirts over the forest floor or glacier worn stone. That essence silently accompanies the pungent smell of deep woods which flows out over the water when the sun has set and downdrafts carry it off the mountain slopes. It's caught somehow in the cool, moist depth of moss and in armies of ferns marching over ledges in incomparable tapestries. It speaks in the romping smile of sunlit water, but just as clearly in that same water enfuried by a storm. It sings in the voice of a thrush and lives in the dark pools that are the eyes of a fawn looking at its new world without fear, only wonder. It emerges from the strange half-vision permitted in fog, mist, or snow and sometimes it's in ghostly fingers of the northern lights when they quiver white, green or crimson in the night sky.

The essence is in the inevitable rhythm nothing has destroyed, a rhythm that is age old yet always new. The essence is something many seek, some, perhaps, without knowing it.

My thanks to many who gave me encouragement, photos, recollections, stories and criticism. These include the late Mrs. Roy Anderson, Tongue Mt.; Mrs. Ann Knapp Chapman, Shelving Rock; Mr. Maitland DeSormo, Saranac Lake; Mr. and Mrs. Sherwood Finley, Fourteen Mile Island; Capt. and Mrs. Martin Fisher, Lake George; Mr. and Mrs. Ernest Granger, Ft. Ann; the late Miss Jane Hebner, Shelving Rock; Margot Wilme Johnson, Truesdale Hill Rd.; the late Mr. Walter Kenworthy, Glens Falls; the late Mrs. William Knapp, Shelving Rock; Mr. and Mrs. G. Owen Knapp, Shelving Rock; Mr. Ed Kreinheder, Warrensburg; Mr. and Mrs. Ralph Lapham, Glens Falls; Mrs. Howard Orcutt, W. Ft. Ann; Mr. George Simon, New York City, the late Miss Helen Simon, Oldwick, N.J.; the late Miss Helen Simpson, Bolton Ldg.; Mr. and Mrs. James Smith, Bolton Ldg.; Miss Pauline Smith, Glens Falls; Mrs. Frank Knapp Sprole, Shelving Rock; Mr. and Mrs. Fred Stiles, South Bay; Mrs. Jesse Stiles, Ft. Ann; Mr. John Stiles, Glens Falls; Mr. Ralph Stiles, Jr., Shelving Rock; Rev. Ernest Van R. Stires, Shelving Rock; Mr. Philip Sullivan, Chestertown; Mrs. Ray Walkup, Glens Falls, the late Mrs. Lucinda White, Hogtown;, and the late Mr. and Mrs. William Steinback, Shelving Rock.

Elsa Steinback
Shelving Rock

Table of Contents

Chapter 1

From Glaciers To A Name

Animals will often turn over a stone to look for food such as grubs or other like tidbits but humans have a habit of doing this with no real reason behind it. Many a person walking the shore, islands or mountain trails along Lake George will pause to rest or wait for a lagging friend and dislodge a stone with a foot, rolling it over with little thought about the idle action. That stone can tell a history to the relatively few who pause to study its composition. They can read thereby the nature of its origin or how it came to lie there. Most walk on not realizing or perhaps caring that the stone is quite possibly among the oldest known rock on the face of the earth. It may have come off a nearby ledge or be a piece of ancient Adirondack mountain top, the mountain having been decapitated by the enormous glaciers of the ice ages. These same glaciers were largely responsible for the magnificently beautiful lake of today.

Geologic ages are comprised of years by the thousand and million fold. In such hardly comprehensible reckoning of time Lake George is considered quite a young lake. This is not true of the mountains which circle it. The Adirondacks of northern New York within whose southern perimeter the lake lies are among the oldest

Ripple mark stone

13

mountains on earth. Their structure and general appearance are evidences of this. The peaks are not ragged and saw-toothed as are those of much younger ranges. The forces with which nature works, cataclysmic or otherwise, have not had time to smooth the latter into such great hoary domes as the Adirondacks present today.

Millions of years before Lake George was born the original Adirondacks were thrust up out of a great inland sea. Geologists speak of this as the Grenville Sea. Its waters once covered vast portions of Canada and northern areas of the United States.

As is true of all oceans, seas and lakes down through the ages this primordial body of water received tons of silt from rivers which drained existing land masses. In time pressure compressed the silts into sandstones, shales and limestones. These quite naturally are called sedimentary rocks. This rock floor of the Grenville Sea eventually buckled and was thrust upward. The action was aided and abetted by a great outpouring of molten matter from deep within the earth. This when cooled became a type of rock known as igneous, namely granites, syenites and gabbros. Both sedimentary and igneous rocks were often vastly altered subsequently by pressures and shiftings. As for example sandstone was changed (or metamorphosed) into quartzite, shale into schist, limestone into marble. Many such types of ancient stone form the Adirondacks, including the Lake George region. The lake's basin, however, was carved out much later.

The great grandfather peaks that were the origional Adirondacks were Alpine sized mountains, far higher than they are today. Once again, when a sinking occurred, the land was washed in part by a sea known as the Cambrian. Again the land mass rose but evidences of that sea can be found along the lake today. These are stones bearing clearly defined ripple marks left by its waters on sand or mud beaches which later became solidified. Local people speak of these stones as "Indian washboards" for they do indeed resemble the galvanized washboards of grand-mothers' days.

The Lake George basin was carved out by another great change which came over the earth's surface not nearly as long ago. Prior to this the lake area had been subjected to extraordinarily violent shiftings, strains, and stresses in the bedrock. Cracks formed along which upheavals and sinkings occurred. The process is known geologically as faulting. It is this faulting which caused two deep troughs to form north and south of the present narrows of the lake, troughs through which rivers began to flow. They drained a mountain barrier which existed at the narrows effectively dividing the watersheds to north and south. The northerly stream drained through a valley west of Rogers Rock while the southbound one followed much the course of today's Northwest Bay Brook winding its way on through the lowlands at Kattskill Bay.

Then there came a time when the continent's temperatures dropped mercilessly downward. Four successive ice ages sent gigantic glacial fingers sprawling over much of its northern regions. Advancing inexorably south out of the arctic the ice covered the countryside to a depth of several thousand feet. In the Adirondacks even mighty Mt. Marcy, the Cloud Splitter, lay buried. The moving, grinding ice tore off the old Adirondack summits and gouged new valleys here as everywhere in its path. It carried with it accumulated rock and debris using these as added abrasives.

When at last temperatures rose again and the ice shield melted back, tons of the debris were left scattered or dumped in masses over land which had been scraped to its bare bones.

The cutting of the ice and subsequent depositing of glacial debris radically altered old watersheds. The debris formed many an effective dam. Here at Lake George the lowlands around Kattskill Bay were thus choked by deposits. The water no longer found an outlet in a southerly direction. Trapped in this way its level continued to rise until it began to flow northward over and around the remnants left by the glaciers of the mountain barrier at the narrows. The water flowed on into the deep northern trough and then, finding the old outlet also blocked by debris, took its way northward via the present outlet. Many of the old ground down mountain summits were left protruding as islands in the new lake. While the lake's shape was now generally established the land around it at first resembled arctic tundra. As temperatures continued to rise other vegetation gradually returned. The above is of course an abridged account of the lake's formation.

Some forms of prehistoric vegetation are still with us today although for the most part very shrunken in size. To visualize what ancient forests were like anyone walking the woods, fields and swamps must imagine the ferns, horsetails, and club mosses (ground pine and cedar)) of today as tree sized plants. Beneath them were the liverworts, mosses, lichens and fungi, all plants whose reproductive processes are quite different from those of the later-developing seed bearers. In the case of ferns for example, parent and offspring do not resemble each other. Like contemporaries of prehistoric origin ferns bear spores, not fertile seeds. When the spore falls to the earth it grows into a small flat green plant called a prothalium. This strange unobtrusive plant produces male sperms and eggs. When the two are washed together by rain or dew fertilization takes place and the resulting plant is a fern like its grandparent.

Lichens, those grey (very rarely green) plants on tree bark, stone or soil are in fact a combination of two plants dependent on each other. They are made up of algae and fungi — the one, in this case, unable to live without the other, each having a specific function. Among the soil dwellers are the minute red-capped lichens commonly called "British Soldiers" and their cousins the "Fairy Cups" with their tiny grey green chalices. (Cladonia cristatella and Chlorophaea).

The origin of the name "Adirondack" is a trifle clouded. There are several theories as to its derivation. Most frequently the word is thought to be from the language of the Mohawks, fiercest of the tribes which made up the great Indian federation known as the Six Nations or Iroquois. Translated it is said to mean "tree or bark eaters". One theory claims it was derisively applied by the Mohawks to tribes of lesser prowess who fled the prime hunting territory of the mountains before Mohawk terrorizing. It may also have been used simply as a name for all other Indian nations although a bit of sarcasm would seem to be implied. There are a few other possible sources of the name.

Whatever the truth may be this much is certain. The name Adirondack was first applied to the mountains in 1837 by Professor Ebenezer Emmons of Williams College. Emmons was an extremely versatile, erudite man who was commissioned to conduct the first survey of the mountains in 1837-38 by New York's governor, William Marcy. On climbing the Adirondacks' highest peak Emmons named it after the governor. A little over a quarter of a century later came the famous and far more extensive survey by Verplank Colvin but the name of the mountain was not changed.

Ferns along the Mountain Road in fall.   Painting by the Author

The water of Lake George is uncommonly clear for the lake has no major inlet and few feeding brooks. Hopefully it will remain so. Most of the water filters down through forest soil and rock to enter the lake as underwater springs. Surface water pours in over ancient rock ledges deepening on its way the colors of the incomparable carpets of mosses and lichens, and ferns. Ruthless early lumbering methods are of the past, the run-offs no longer carry with them masses of silt and debris, the mountain slopes are once more covered with forests where duff and loam lie deep enough to absorb and thereby nourish. Man, albeit slowly, is learning that wilderness is as necessary to him as food and water for it nourishes in a different way.

No highway has ever touched the narrows of the lake, the area of its climactic loveliness. An old lumber road runs for a distance along the eastern shore of the region but it gets there as torturously as it did when first cut over a century ago. The road climbs up and over high ridges to the east to drop down to the lake near a little half-loaf of a mountain undoubtedly worked over by the glaciers. It is called Shelving Rock and stretches a long beak out to pinch the lake together forming the southeastern entrance to the narrows. The road ends suddenly with no other egress possible and is closed to vehicular traffic before it reaches the lakeshore since it cuts across private property. Its northern reaches are for hikers only. Once a part of its course ran past several small farms, that is to say small by today's measure. They are gone as are most small farms everywhere. Farm pastures and fields, stone walls and foundations are overgrown and almost if not entirely lost to sight as are the foundations and grounds of five hotels which existed in the narrows in the latter part of the 19th century. Today most of the narrows' shores and mountains are state land within the Adirondack Park.

The following pages in part tell the story of these hotels and the ways of life which surrounded them. Bound closely with their history are the tremendous changes brought about by the age of steam. Steamboats and railroads made access to the lake, for that matter to the whole Adirondack region, ever faster and easier. The narrows hotels were similar to most Adirondack resorts of the time. Families returned season after season to their favorite resort for the restless, questing automobile was a thing of the future. Autos, along with motor boats and airplanes, were to alter the habits of vacationers as the 20th century progressed. Through them people achieved a mobility never before known.

In the 19th century it was the steamboats which formed the lifeline along the lake. Roads were bumpy and dusty and stagecoaches spine-jarring vehicles here as elsewhere. The Tongue Mountain Range at the narrows had only a barely passable road over its steep slopes. To all intents and purposes there was no road connecting the two ends of the lake.

The first steamboat appeared on this lake in 1817, a scant ten years after a man named Robert Fulton proved that a vessel could actually be propelled by a steam driven engine. Fulton was not, as is often supposed, the first to design and attempt to operate such a boat. The idea was conceived much earlier and even tried out before the Revolution but never with great success. Experiments were made by the famous John Stevens of Castle Point, Hoboken, lawyer, engineer and inventor. He launched a steamboat in 1801 but it didn't live up to expectations.

Stevens' brother-in-law was one of the most powerful men in the young nation. This was Robert Livingston whose large estate, Clermont, lay along the banks of the

Hudson. One time member of the Continental Congress and later first Chancellor of the State of New York it was in the latter capacity that he had administered the first presidential oath of office to George Washington. Livingston had other irons in the fire one of which was to gain absolute monopoly of river traffic. He shifted his backing to young Robert "Toot" Fulton whose design for a steamboat, though still a gamble, bid fair to be successful. (Fulton also married into the Chancellor's family.)

When the boat became actuality it was known as The North River Steamboat and did become the first such boat to operate with commercial success, but the name "Clermont", by which she has gone down in history was not applied until both boat and designer were gone. At the time, in spite of Livingston's faith in the venture, many looked upon a steam driven boat as "a backwoods sawmill mounted on a scow and set afire"! The contraption, they felt, would soon meet a fiery death!

Fulton's boat triumphantly made the trip from New York to Albany in the running time of 32 hours. Fulton was forever afterward known as the father of steamboating but her first engineer lost his place in history. He was so overcome by her success that he got gloriously drunk on reaching Albany and was promptly fired.

Shortly thereafter John Stevens' sidewheeler "Phoenix" ran with equal success but by then the Livingston-Fulton monopoly had been established. Stevens' boat eventually sought business on the Delaware, becoming on the trip down the first steamboat to challenge the sea.

Knowledge of the power of steam was not confined to this country. Shortly after the advent of the steamboat came the operation of a commercially feasible steam locomotive in England. Again, John Stevens had been experimenting with the idea in America. It was about then that the great anthracite coal beds of Pennsylvania were discovered. "Hard coal" was still however a rather unknown quantity. In fact the first loads to reach Philadelphia were almost mobbed by irate citizens who claimed the black "stones" were a hoax! Nevertheless two brothers named Wurts went right ahead and bought up all the coal lands they could for 50 cents to 3 dollars an acre. By 1823 they had formed a company they named The Delaware and Hudson Canal Company for a canal had been dug from Honesdale, Pa. to Rondout on the Hudson to bring the coal to markets. Once more the little company put faith in its own judgment when it sent to England for one of the new locomotives. This was an odd looking little affair which bore the impressive name, "Stourbridge Lion". On arrival it went by barge to the coal country to be the first commercially operated locomotive on the continent. The company itself grew larger and larger as years went by until it became the Delaware and Hudson Railroad System whose operations served lakes George and Champlain, even in time absorbing the steamboat companies on both lakes. It's history, too, that railroad trackage spread out like a giant silver webb through the 19 century. In 1869 two threads of shining rails met at Promontory Point Utah to link the continent from east and west.

More than two centuries earlier in the year 1642 the first white man known to have set eyes on Lake George was brought to its shores as a captive of Indian warriors. He wore the black robes of the Jesuit Order for he had dedicated his life to the service of God. French missionaries of his type were penetrating deep into the wilderness of the new world hoping to carry their faith to the Indian peoples. In that year this slender wiry man was tortured and mutilated by his captors but escaped death when a kindly Dutch trader bought him from his captors. He returned to

France for a time but then voyaged back across the sea to continue his work. In 1646 he stood once again beside the lake whose waters were so crystal clear. It chanced to be the Eve of the Festival of Corpus Christi. In honor of the day he named the lovely lake "Lac du St. Sacrament" (Lake of The Blessed Sacrament). The priest's name was Isaac Joques. He was soon to die a martyr's death at the hands of those he strove to convert. Father Joques was canonized by the Catholic Church in 1930.

A statue of St. Joques stands at the head of the lake today looking out over its waters. However the name he gave it was not to be perpetuated. A little over a hundred years after his coming it would be changed. When France and Britain went to war over control of the new world a soldier of His British Majesty George II arrived at the lake head. He was General Sir William Johnson. The general had his field desk brought to him and wrote:

"I am encamped at this lake which the French call St. Sacrament but I have given the name George, not only in honor of His Majesty but to ascertain his undoubted dominion here."

Stourbridge Lion.

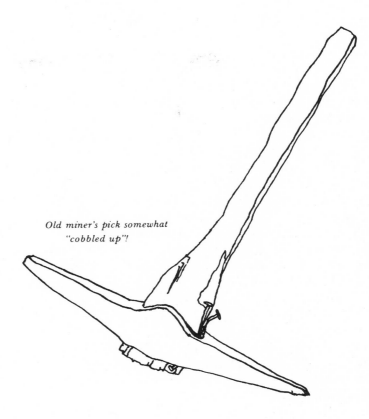

Old miner's pick somewhat
"cobbled up"!

Chapter 2

Fact and Folklore

The material for this book comes from many sources. There are history books of course, there still exist old posters and guide books to the area dating far back into the 19th century. Some of the most informative of the latter are the yearly guides published from the 1870s into the early 20th century by Seneca Ray Stoddard of Glens Falls, photographer and raconteur extraordinaire. Along with printed words however are stories handed down by word of mouth told to me by people who had known people who remembered at first hand events, places and bygone ways of life along the lake. Quite naturally these last always bring a dash of coloring like no other. Consequently regular walks through history are mixed with random scoots via local folklore. This leaves the nice choice to the reader of believing all that follows verbatim or enjoying some of it with a smile. Actually a bit of embroidery in a tale is as much a part of a countryside as pure historical veracity. If it gives nothing else it adds flavor like a dash of salt. Most certainly that dash of salt is far from unusual in Adirondack stories!

There's a tale, sworn to as truth, of an episode which brought about the end of a local iron furnace southeast of a spot known as Hogtown. Hogtown itself is now a ghost town although the area still carries the name. The location is a mountainous one roughly between the old town of Ft. Ann and Lake George just south of the narrows. Hogtown's inhabitants dwindled away quite some years ago leaving only their church building, a tiny red schoolhouse (since deceased) and miles of stone pasture walls which now disappear into forest. Some folks always hated the name Hogtown feeling it lacked dignity and distinction and thus must reflect on the inhabitants. There were just as many who brushed aside such qualmishness as nonsense and defended the name because it was a natural outcome of utilitarianism. The facts are that Hogtown was located in an area where nature had provided many wild nut trees. Farmers from all around thriftily drove their hogs to the environs in fall to fatten them on nature's bounty.

Just when Hogtown saw its first settler I do not know but the ubiquitous lumbermen advanced early into the prime timberland of the mountains. Farmers followed the lumberjacks. Eventually two roads converged at the heighth of land where Hogtown grew and went on as one toward the lakeshore to the west. Meanwhile the area developed another industry namely the mining and smelting of precious iron ore. The ore bed was discovered near Podunk Pond (now Lake Nebo) in 1823. It was a bonanza for the early settlers because all manner of indispensable farm implements, logging tools, household pots and pans, horse and oxen shoes, anchors and chains could be forged locally. Such things were difficult and costly to get from afar. Iron not needed nearby was shipped elsewhere via the fine new Champlain Canal which also opened in 1823. Canals were the coming thing throughout the land as everyone agreed in those early years of the 19th century.

"19th century Champlain Canal kerosene channel lantern."

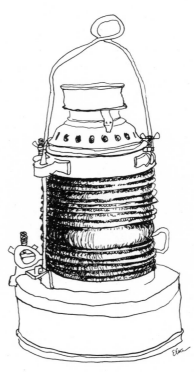

22

As miners blasted and dug the ore out of its mountainside a blast furnace was built a few miles away. The structure resembled the more famous one built for the Adirondack Iron Works and Messrs. MacIntyre and Henderson at Tahawus. The local one stands beside Mt. Hope Brook which drains eastward into Lake Champlain's South Bay.

Around this furnace, or "stack" as it was often called, a settlement grew referred to as Mt. Hope after the mountain on one side of the narrow brook valley. Straining teams hauled the ore several mountainous miles from the mine to the stack. The circuitous roads often became quagmires bogging down the heavy wagons. Slag from the furnace was soon used as ballast on the worst stretches. Chunks of this can still be picked up. It's an opaque, glassy substance, purple, green, or more rarely a lovely colbalt blue. Bits of charcoal are sometimes embedded in it for charcoal was used in place of coal all through the north country in the iron smelters of that day. Coal simply was not procurable. With men employed at the mine, others at the stack, still others found work and profit burning hardwoods into the charcoal. Pits were dug in the ground, the wood carefully stacked inside and allowed to smoulder for several days, with a minimum of draft of course.

Both mine and stack belong to history now but both can still be visited after walks along the old roads which have shrunken to trails and would seem to ramble off to nowhere. The mine tunnels open gaping, pitch black mouths on a forested mountainside. Drill marks are clearly seen in the uncompromising stone out of which the tunnels were hewn. Water drips constantly in the darkness inside. It forms icy pools there whose depth is an uncertainty. Along the shrunken wagon road outside a few piles of somewhat sparkling grey-black ore lie awaiting wagons which will not come again. The ore is heavy and supposed to be of very fine grade.

In the V-like valley below Mt. Hope the great stack stands silent and almost forgotten. One coming on it unexpectedly might at first be startled at the wonder of a medieval castle tower inexplicably here in a northern New York forest. Around it are depressions that were cellars of homes and stores. The enormous stones of which the squared and massive furnace was built remain firmly in place because of sheer weight and balance. Getting them set as they are long before cranes, bulldozers or other great modern machines existed or were even dreamed of represents hours of sweat and toil and ingenious know-how.

Officially the mine was known as the Wiggins Mine. It fed the maw of the big stack for many years throughout the 19th century. The exact date of the mine's demise I do not know but the story involving the end of operations at the furnace is local lore. According to the latter the end came abruptly.

When it happened and for some years previously, one indispensable individual knew most about the care of the huge stack, when the pure iron had been separated from the slag and when the mass should be drawn off. Over him was a foreman who had charge of the whole works but this man didn't have the specialized knowledge about the furnace itself. One year the two of them each professed ownership of an exceptionally fine, fat pig. They didn't quite come to blows but the foreman took the pig. The genie of the stack was choleric with rage. He pronounced a dire dictum.

"At four o'clock this day," he bellowed pointing at the stack, "ye'll see the last smoke come outta thar ye'll ever be seein' for I'm quittin' as of now an' I hain't comin' back nohow!"

Depart he did, leaving the mass to harden within. At four o'clock, almost to the minute folks said, a last wisp of smoke curled from the massive furnace to drift off into history. With their livelihood gone folks had to pick up and move elsewhere. It was indeed a costly pig if the story so told ended the life of Mt. Hope Furnace!

All this probably happened somewhere in the late eighteen hundreds. By then several summer hotels existed along the shores of the narrows of Lake George as we shall see later. The road through Hogtown ran on down to this region for lumbermen hadn't stopped at that settlement! It's not likely that many summer visitors walked the long miles uphill to Hogtown. Neither did they discover the mining or smelting operations going on not too far beyond. The hotels were part of a world once again removed from frontier days even as mine and stack were removed a shade less far. The English spoken in the mountains itself kept expression and connotations of an earlier day, some of them quite charming and even now in use. The two worlds met at the hotels for some local people found employment there. They seldom met behind the mountains. Times and customs changed less quickly there. In the early memory of people living today there were children who grew to adulthood in the little world behind the mountains before they glimpsed the larger world a scant ten miles or so down the road.

One day not so very long ago several of these youngsters went with their father to pick blueberries on the upper slopes where Mt. Buck, once better known as Deer Pasture Mt., raises its semi-bald dome just southeast of the narrows. Hogtown lies in the high country behind it. The rocky upper regions of the mountain have more than once burned over rather mysteriously. It is true of course that blueberries thrive in burned-over areas. The summit of Buck is still a good place for berrypickers. The boys' father was still a ways below when one of the lads reached the top. His eyes widened as far down on the lake below he saw one of the great white sidewheelers heading sedately toward the narrows. The boy let a big yell out of him;

"Paw! Paw! C'm here! C'm here, quick!"

The frightened father ran up the trail as fast as he could thinking his son had met with an accident, possibly a rattlesnake. When he breathlessly gained the summit he found the boy jumping up and down in high excitement and pointing downward.

"Jesus Paw! Jesus! Lookit that big ship!" Never in his wildest imaginings had the child conceived of so large a boat!

It wasn't only that boy who would remember the big side-wheelers as something very special. When they were suddenly gone from the scene, we who all our earlier lives had also reacted to the aura of them, the excitement they generated, knew that something gallant, gay and proud had sailed into the past forever. We had lost time worn friends. Much of the history of those boats is woven into what follows for they were an indispensable part of life along the lake for well over a century.

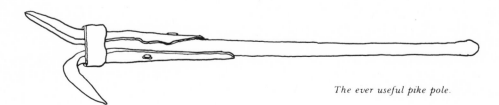

The ever useful pike pole.

24

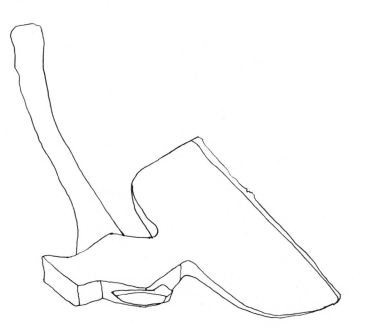

Chapter 3

Settlement Lumber and Steam

The gigantic, abrading glaciers of the ice ages carved out the basin of the future Lake George into one of potentially great beauty. However it was not the eventual fulfillment of that potential which put the lake in a prominent place in the early history of this country. Nor did it bring the first settlers to its shores.

The lake forms part of an almost continuous natural water route from Manhattan Island to Montreal. In early days this provided far the best way for travel, warlike or otherwise. Consisting of the Hudson River, Lakes George and Champlain and the Richelieu River, the waterway was used by Indian peoples long before European colonists arrived. Then it became of vital importance to British colonies to south and east and the French to the north. Armies of both nations used it in the eventual and inevitable struggle for domination of the 'new world' which was known as the French and Indian War. Forts were built along the waterway since both France and Britain knew that control of it might lead to ultimate victory. There were successive British forts at the head of Lake George, namely William Henry, Gage, and George. Across the lake's outlet overlooking Champlain the French built Fort Carillon later known as mighty Ticonderoga.

Thus Lake George once saw brilliantly uniformed armies of the old world. The bright colors of their uniforms with flashing accoutrements were ill adapted to frontier warfare. They made easy targets. Colonial scouts such as Robert Rogers' famous Rangers knew better. Their unobtrusive dress enabled them to slip about unseen and unheard as they skirmished through the no-man's-land Lake George became. Such stealthy bands of both sides were abroad in all seasons although major campaigning was suspended in the rigorous winters. The poor devils left to garrison the forts could only curse the lonely, God-forsaken wilderness that was their lot.

During the Revolution the lake again saw conflicts but not to as large an extent. When Britain put into action a strategic plan to cut the rebellious colonies in two the commanding general, "Gentleman Johnny" Burgoyne, took his army southward from Ticonderoga by way of Skenesborough (now Whitehall). This is the route of the present Champlain Canal. His defeat and surrender at Old Saratoga was a great turning point of that war.

When the War of 1812 again brought threat via the north country men from the tiny new settlements along Lake George joined others in a march to the Battle of Plattsburgh. A company was commanded by Captain Pliny Pierce of Bolton. One day some years later he died after a fall from his horse on a steep hill near home. The road is still called "Break Neck Hill Road."

There are fine museums today in the reconstructed forts at both ends of Lake George. History comes alive there. It is also true that relics of the wars and of earlier Indian inhabitants of the area can be found outside of museum showcases. They can turn up along the shores and islands and on the lake's bottom. The objects may be arrow or spear points, celts, cannon and musket balls, pewterware, uniform buttons or coins, pottery shards, rusted firearms, even perhaps cannon and vessels. Sometimes I have found such things myself. Holding them I've wondered who last touched them? Who made or used them? Did some find the mark for which they were intended? I feel I'm touching history with my hands.

An account of a voyage through the lake in 1776 was written by Rev. John Carroll who was travelling with his brother Charles, Samuel Chase and Benjamin Franklin. They were en route to examine the state of American forces in Canada. Their boat was a batteau with a blanket for a sail. Carroll wrote of the lake; ". . . its shores are remarkably steep and rocky . . . and are covered with pine and cedar, this country is wild and appears utterly incapable of cultivation, it is fine deer country and likely to remain so for I think it never will be inhabited"!

Thomas Jefferson, James Madison and George Washington were among notables who toured the lake after the Revolution. Jefferson wrote to his daughter, "Lake George . . . is the most beautiful water I ever saw". But this was frontier country still, best remembered as a bloody battleground and an area of uncompromising wilderness. It would be some years before its beauty would become an economic asset. The first settlers came for a far more tangible asset than beauty. This was lumber!

The great forests just to the south had already felt the bite of ax and saw. In colonial days the tallest, straightest trees became by rigid law the property of His British Majesty's Navy. A settlement called Wing's Falls, ten miles south of the lake's head predated the Revolution. It later became "Glens" Falls and grew as a lumber town since it was located on the banks of the high born Hudson River which floated

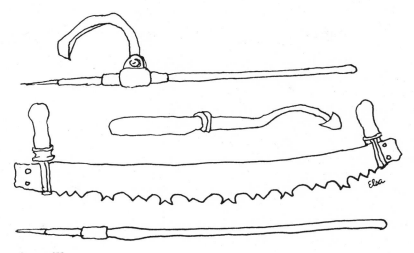

the timber to its mill.

By the late 1790s settlers had come to the shores of Lake George. Some who served during the colonial wars doubtless remembered the prime timber on the lake's mountains. The first real settlement is said to have been at Bolton, ten miles downlake. The plows of those settlers, grating against innumerable boulders and stones left by the ancient glaciers, cleared just enough of the difficult terrain to ensure food. Then the men headed into the forest and the great timbers began to fall. Founded in the late 1790s Bolton boasted of some twelve lumber mills by 1810!

A man often mentioned in connection with the early days there was Father Paul, a full-blooded Indian of the Mohican tribe. Raised in the Christian faith he had become a "duely licensed minister". He arrived in the area shortly after the Revolution and there "preached on the Sabbath, shared the early settlers joys, buried their dead, and consoled them in times of affliction." Father Paul unfortunately fell victim to a curse introduced by his white brothers. He became an alcoholic. Still and all an early settler described him thus; "His broad high-cheekboned face was spread with an habitual smile of benevolence . . . he was good to us and ministered from house to house and on the Sabbath in Holy Things. He had his weakness . . . we know it . . . at length Father Paul went from us, whether falling a victim to his habit, dying in a poorhouse, or escaping to some distant haunt I could never learn. The general belief is that he died alone, that he built a hut far down the lake . . . where the beetling cliffs of Tongue Mt. almost shut off passage."* There is indeed no record of Father Paul's death.

Near the ruins of the old forts at the head of the lake a settlement named Caldwell sprang up (now Lake George Village). The name honored a prominent resident, General James Caldwell, who held the patent to several thousand acres of the vicinity. There in early days a brisk lumber business was also carried on although for lack of brooks with the essential water power most timber was rafted to Ticonderoga. Caldwell did boast of a few so-called "thunder shower" mills. In 1832 the Glens Falls Feeder branch of the Champlain Canal was completed and lumbering increased along the Hudson River and decreased at the head of Lake George. Slowly the resort business took its place along the lake. One unkind wag was heard to say, "The natives now seem to live mostly on fish and strangers"!

*Quoted from History of Warren County — 1885

A third settlement along the lake was first known as Rochester. In 1808 the name changed to Hague.

Pioneer lumbermen saw so much forest on every side that harvesting of trees seemed limitless. They chopped and sawed and left a devastation of stumps and tangled branches. When lightning struck or floods washed down the denuded slopes the havoc was worse but no one cared. In time many a mountain along the lake showed its rocky skeleton clearly or was blackened by unchecked fires.

Until the early 1900s logs were skidded to the lakeshore and there formed into huge rafts or "booms". These were floated to mills by skilled boatmen, men with good knowledge of the lake's currents and moods. The lake is inclined to sudden violence as many have found out. Early in this century the practice was stopped by law. The danger to vacationers of escaped timbers was too great.

The forested mountains of the lake's lovely narrows didn't escape the ax and saw. Remains of a lumber camp are still traceable near beautiful Paradise Bay. The camp was known as Lyons Clearing and there are still depressions where its cabins stood. Here and there can be found an old apple tree and there was until recently a pile of rusted horse and ox shoes. It's covered now by forest duff.

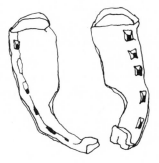

Each ox hoof wore shoes like this.

Oxen are immensely powerful beasts. They were often used in old Adirondack lumber camps. Incidentally they must be shod with two shoes on every foot since they are of course cloven-hooved. The great animals were still used in the woods within the memory of people I've known, one of whom was Lucinda White. She was the daughter of an oldtime lumberman, a heritage she wore as a proud mantle all her life. Being a practical woman, when power saws and 'dozers came along she didn't exactly scorn them but there was something in her eyes kindled by the memory of ax, saw, and the straining teams, brawn and muscle of earlier days. She often related that her father had the last team of oxen used in the mountains back of the narrows.

Like a contemporary, John Stiles, Lucinda found employment most of her working life on the great Knapp Estate which in the early years of this century followed the era of the narrows hotels. She was born in the little settlement around the blast furnace at Mt. Hope. During Lucinda's childhood and youth lumbering was a major industry still in those mountains. She herself learned the use of ax, pike pole and peavey at a tender age and could handle them with accuracy and almost the strength of a man almost until her death. As a matter of fact she was never

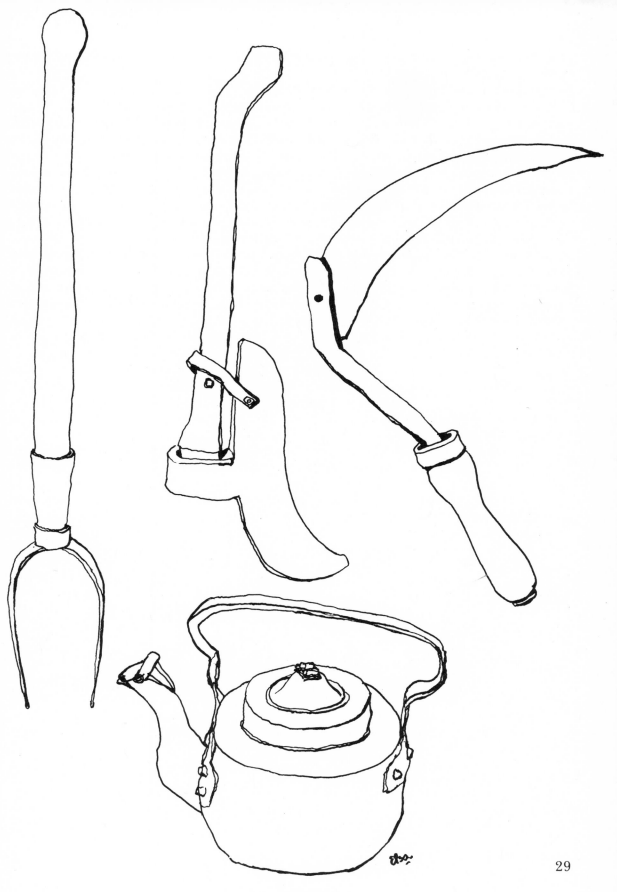

Part of early life here.

29

happier than when she could pick up the ol' ax and head for the woods or lumber pile. "Jes 'holler if'n I'm needed at the house for somethin', I seen some wood (or tree or bush) as needs cuttin' yonder an' I aim to git it done!" And away she'd go with great joy. Many a time she'd sigh on seeing tall straight pines on the Knapp property, then remark wistfully how many fine board feet stood firmly rooted there.

It was Lucinda who told of the little Hogtown church in its active days. Whenever an itinerant preacher came along to hold a service there she'd go with her folks and all the rest of the countryside, done up in Sunday best. Wagons, horses and carriages crowded the churchyard and often the building would be so full the menfolk had to stand outside and listen at the windows.

Young Lucinda grew into a strong woman, square-set and handsome with red-gold hair that didn't belie her nature. She rode her horse on the mountain road, folks said, with that hair a-flyin'! Her strength was abetted by a faith in the Will of the Lord and her own ability to meet life square on. She learned to go about daily tasks at a measured pace knowing that energy is often wasted by too much speed. She had her vanities to be sure but there was often a twinkle in her blue eyes which could foretell moments of pure impishness. She had one predilection which caused John or other co-workers some concern. Seeing any unsightly mess of brush, a forelorn old building or the like she would set out to have what she called "a burnin'." How could such things be more satisfactorily disposed of than by fire? She was sure that fire was easy to control if one knew how and no one ever convinced her otherwise. Sensing a "burnin" was coming on John and others kept noses to the breeze and Indian pumps at hand. She was just as ready to go out and fight a forest fire armed with ax and broom.

John often went to fetch her after her day off at Hogtown which became her most beloved spot on earth and "home". She knew the idiosyncrasies of her co-workers as they did hers. In consequence she would warn a fellow passenger on occasion; "Better hang on, kid, for John's agoin' down the mounting!" John, of whom more will follow in another chapter, sometimes drove with a sort of joyful abandon because there were other things along the way of more interest than the well known road. He'd read the signs, where a deer had crossed recently and whether buck or doe, where a hen partridge had led her brood, or possibly a strange tire mark warranted investigation later. Perhaps he felt that the car, like the wagon horses of his youth, should know the way by itself.

For two winters Lucinda, in her later years, went to Arizona as housekeeper-companion. The desert fazed her not at all. She maintained that up home in Hogtown there were woodpeckers and a church steeple and in Arizona there were woodpeckers too and cacti (Saguaros) just like church steeples and where one could find both, one could find peace too. Thus she took her measure of the arid land but when taken to see Frank Lloyd Wright's Taliesin West she had reservations. A young East Indian student was conducting the tour that day and pointed out the recessed windows which supposedly kept out wind and dust without glass. Lucinda shook her head. She told him,

"Say you should tell Mr. Wright I seen an ad of Sears Roebuck in the paper today. They're havin' a sale of windows an' he should march right down there an' git some so's he can finish this place!"

Flying home alone one spring (before the jet age), her plane met severe enough turbulence that passengers were given the option of continuing by train. Lucinda elected to stay aboard for many on the plane were violently airsick and she could be of help to them. The lady from Hogtown had made the transition from ox team to airplane in a few strides.

In her later years, when I knew her, Lucinda seldom spoke of her husband Will White. He had been gone for many years. They both came to work on the Knapp Estate in the early 1900s. One freezing cold day Will and three other men capsized in the narrows. One man drowned and Will contracted pneumonia, which proved fatal. It was while looking out over those same waters that she said to me not so many years ago, and without concern or sadness;

"Reckon time's acomin' rather soon when this ol' lady'll git in her canoe and paddle off".

She died in her beloved Hogtown not long afterward nor did she have to linger as an invalid. This would have been intolerable. It is said of her, and not only by me, that in her long, useful life no friend or stranger, rich or poor or middlin' who needed help was ever turned away by this indomitable lady from what she herself always called "them mountings were Hogtown be"!

Log Bay at Shelving Rock acquired its name in the days when great timber off the nearby slopes was skidded down the rollbank to the south to be piled on the ice in the bay until spring breakup. Then chained logs across the bay's two entrances kept the timber from escaping until it was formed into rafts and floated away to the mills. Near the turn of the century someone was careless and the mass of logs broke free during a storm to be scattered far and wide in the lake. A small steamboat spent the summer searching them out but boating was somewhat hazardous that season!

Lumber days left another heritage. Many lumber roads and skidways are hiking trails today. Among those in the narrows is the unconscionably steep trail which climbs the notch between Erebus and Black mountains. It was recut and extended to a lovely pond named Fishbrook when the area became part of the George Knapp estate. A brook whose course the trail follows downward to the lake vanishes underground not far above the shore doubtless the source of an underwater spring. I discovered this for myself one day only to learn that John Stiles and others knew it since time began as they did many of my happy "discoveries". By then however I was beginning to get the hang of such things as which big pine among some thousands of its kin on Shelving Rock might be meant as marking a fine deer runway. While esoteric, such landmarks are in another sense commonplace if one uses one's head the right way.

When settlements came to be established along the lake in the early 1800s fear of the mighty Iroquois was over. The tribes had sided with the British during the Revolution and had felt American retribution. Forts at the head of the lake had either been destroyed or lay in ruins. Even mighty Ticonderoga on Champlain was forgotten by all but the thrifty settlers of the area. They'd begun to cart if off stone by stone, casement by casement for where could building materials be acquired more easily and cheaply? Some of it was hauled across Champlain to Larrabee's Point, Vermont. The picturesque old warehouse still standing there near the ferry is said to be of such Ticonderoga stone. A ferry at that place has been operated since early colonial days, probably one of the few enterprises of those times which survives to this day. (A modern diesel tug and a cable now guide the ferry across.) As for the bits and pieces of the old fort they were hauled across the ice in winter by teams and sleighs, the drivers being paid all of $1 for a day's work! There was no thought given then to the fort's value as an historic landmark. The wars were too recently over, the settlements were young and youth does not tend to look backward.

On Lake Champlain two brothers weren't looking backward either. Their name was Winans. Some claim that one of them assisted in the building of Robert Fulton's Clermont. Whether true or not, in 1808, only one year after the Clermont's initial run the brothers laid the keel of a steamboat on the large lake. In 1809 this became the second commercially operated steamboat in the world. Her scheduled run from St. Johns to Whitehall was supposed to be of 24 hours duration but breakdowns or adverse winds (when sailing ships could easily outrun her) often made the time much longer. Yet in spite of the laughter of sailboat captains and jokes at her expense the age of steam had come to the north country and would not be turned back. The best speed attained by the little steamer "Vermont" was about 5 MPH in spite of which the public took note. An early account tells that soon there were even "old lady passengers who continually made anxious inquiries as to whether all was safe? How hot did they keep that furnace?" And they direly kept forecasting an accident in which passengers "would have a choice between death by hot water on deck or cold water below"!

To expedite the little steamer's voyages, wood was cut and stacked at various points along the lakeshore. She churned and chuffed up and down Champlain valiantly until 1815. In that year a connecting rod suddenly broke loose. It pierced her hull and she sank. Nevertheless people had come to have more faith in steam and a second steamboat was under construction on Champlain when the War of 1812 again saw the British attacking out of Canada. A young lieutenant named MacDonough was dispatched by the stripling American Navy to build and command a fleet on the big lake. He promptly commandeered the new hull but feeling that steam was still far too erratic and untried for a fighting ship, converted the boat into a sloop. Under the name "Ticonderoga" she fought with honor in the Battle of Plattsburgh Bay. Her hull has been recovered from the lake bottom and is on display at the museum at Whitehall, N.Y. Almost a century later the same name was given the last great sidewheeler launched for service on Champlain. (1906) This one rests today at the famous museum at Shelburne, Vt.

John Winans wasn't discouraged by the fate of the little "Vermont". He salvaged her engine and boilers and some years later turned up with them at Caldwell on Lake George. He hoped to interest leading citizens in a steamboat for this lake. He got the backing he needed and a steamer was launched at Caldwell in 1817. She bore the name "James Caldwell" in honor of one of her chief sponsors. It was a rather quaint looking vessel for the smoke stack was built of bricks! Skippered by Winans himself she puffed along at about the speed a good oarsman could row but the oarsman could keep rowing while she quite frequently stopped puffing because something broke down. The countryside came to observe her but some folks, seeing smoke and sparks belching from her stack, vowed that this new contraption could only have been built "with the connivance of the Evil One!" They were even more convinced when lightning struck her the first season but she survived this only to burn at her pier in 1821.

In spite of her balkiness the little James Caldwell had a notable claim to fame other than being the first of her kind on this lake. One of her passengers was a very portly gentleman who noted the lake's shores and islands carefully from her deck. A few years later he used these observations in his most famous novel. It was pub-

The little James Caldwell looked something like this.

lished in 1826 and entitled "The Last of The Mohicans". The portly one had been James Fenimore Cooper.

With the exception of a very few years steamboats served the lake from that time on until the 1930s. Although business was better on Champlain in the early days another steamboat was launched at Caldwell in 1824. This was "The Mountaineer" whose construction was so unusual that every account of her mentions it. Few add that she was painted to resemble the flag in stripes of red, white and blue. Her structure somewhat resembled that of a basket. The inner and outer planking ran from stem to stern while a layer between ran from keel to gunwale. Furthermore she was longer and narrower than her predecessor which caused her to frolic through the water in a sinuous manner comparable to that of an eel. It didn't bother Captain Larabee, her skipper, who had a mind to set speed records. In fact he hated to stop along the way let alone slow down very much. Male passengers literally had to catch the boat by having themselves rowed out at the expected time, then as she slowed only a mite, transferring as best they could to a dingy towed by the steamer. This was then hauled alongside for boarding. In justice to the good captain the feat was not required of ladies, in fact 'tis said he stopped quite readily for them!

Even while the age of steam was thus struggling in its infancy rough lumbermen's lodging houses along the lake began to find some profit in sprucing themselves up a bit for tourists. Among the first was the later famous Mohican House at Bolton. It had begun as a tavern around 1802. At the time a small store stood at the pier nearby on the lakeshore. Rumor always had it that under its floor goods were hidden which had been smuggled down from Canada by way of the lakes.

The steamer Mountaineer was followed by the William Caldwell, named after James Caldwell's son. She was larger with double the horsepower of the earlier two boats. A lad who was to become a well known lake captain got a job aboard her as fireman at the age of fifteen. His name was Elias Harris. The Caldwell's master was the same speedy Captain Larabee who often sent the boy in the boat's yawl to pick up passengers. It would seem by then he'd become a little resigned to passenger comfort! Harris published his memoirs after his retirement in 1903. In them he stated that at that early date there were "but two piers, viz Bolton and Hague between the two ends of the lake". The practice of picking up passengers from waiting rowboats was not confined to Lake George, it was fairly common practice because of lack of landings although Captain Larabee's earlier desire for speed and the gymnastic feats required to get aboard in consequence of this were distinctly a part of the Wm. Caldwell's routine voyages!

Tourist traffic was on the increase and posters appeared advertising steamboat schedules which allowed passengers time at the foot of the lake to visit the ruins of Fort Ticonderoga and dine at "The Ticonderoga Hotel". That building had been the home of the Pell family and would subsequently be so again as it still is. The old fort itself had finally become recognized as of great historic note. Some passengers continued northward via the Lake Champlain steamers, others returned southward via the Lake George boat. A line of stage coaches owned by a Captain Baldwin operated between the two lakes passing through Ticonderoga. Some time later a spur line of the D&H Railroad replaced the coaches.

The young fireman Elias Harris rose to the rank of pilot on the next Lake George steamboat. This was The John Jay, built in 1850. She was the only one of the Line ever to know fatalities among passengers. She met a tragic ending. In 1856 off Friends Point near Hague she caught fire. Her pilot emereged a hero, for with tiller ropes burned away and blinded by smoke and steam from exploding boilers, he groped his way to the stern and shipped the tiller hoping to steer the boat to a beach. This was not to be. With no visibility the boat struck rocks and rebounded into deep water. Crew and passengers busily tossed floatable objects overboard for non-swimmers to cling to but six passengers drowned. The steamer burned to the waterline and sank.

There was a local character known as "Old Dick" who had been riding the boat frequently with a display he calc'lated would be of enormous interest to tourists. Whether it was is a moot question. The display consisted of a glass topped box full of live rattlesnakes. Old Dick was an expert snake hunter as others have been before and since. He carefully lettered a sign which he placed on his box. It read: "Admittance Sixpence Site, children half price or nothin". He later added: "In this box ar a rattell snaik hoo was kecht on Black Mounting. He is 7 yrs. old last Guly"!

Dick and his 'snaikes' were aboard when the Jay burned. In the confusion someone heaved the box overboard and a little girl clung to it till it drifted safely ashore while the startled snakes got their heads out of a trap door which had opened. The child was not hurt.

Another account of the tragedy stated that "a young man living nearby threw off his outer clothing, saved six persons...and while he was doing it some public spirited person stole his watch"! So much for the vagaries of human nature...and of 'snaikes'!

The William Caldwell

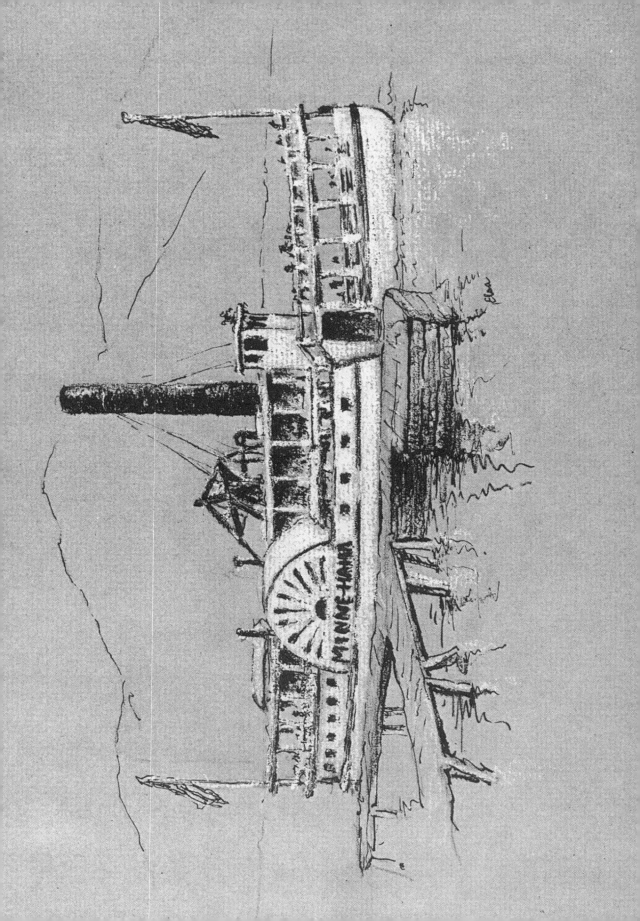

Chapter 4

The Minne

When the John Jay burned the struggling steamboat company had nothing left but a pier. They had to pull themselves together and determine their future before another season came 'round. Somehow the hard-put board of the little company scraped together the $20,000 needed to build an adequate vessel, one which would satisfy the increasing numbers and sophistication of the travelling public and carry more freight as well. It was decided to salvage the engine and boilers of the Jay for the new boat. Her keel was laid near Caldwell. The resulting steamer was said to be weighted with "a heavier mortgage than any load she could carry" but launch her the company did in the spring of 1857.

With an overall length of 144 ft. she was a graceful boat, a side-wheeler which proved to be the prototype of all to follow her on this lake until the steamboat era ended. She had two decks, the upper one open forward and covered aft and could handle about 400 passengers. There was a link with the past in that she was the last woodburner requiring, incidentally, about six cords for the round trip of the lake daily. Her successors would burn coal more readily obtainable by then from the great D&H coal fields.

The Minne-Ha-Ha [from old photo]

In choosing the boat's name the company followed a suddenly popular custom. A Massachusetts poet whose name is a byword, not only in American homes. but throughout the world was then publishing his work. It received quick acclaim. One of the most famous poems appeared in 1855, the story of a great Indian Chief whose name was Hiawatha. From its popular text innumberable boats, large and small, as well as summer bungalows, trails and camps received Indian names and the custom went on for many years! The poet was Henry Wadsworth Longfellow.

Longfellow did not originate the character of Hiawatha whatever the embellishments of his imagination may have been. The legend of Hiawatha is actual Indian lore, its succinct facts being that the great chief was of miraculous birth sent by Indian gods to lead Indian peoples to a better way of life on earth. Chief Hiawatha chose "the loveliest of Dakotah women, Minne-Ha-Ha" to be his wife. The translation of the name is "Laughing Water." Showing imagination of their own the steamboat company's board chose to christen the new boat "Minne-Ha-Ha".

The steamer was soon known affectionately along the lake as "The Minne". Through twenty years of active service she became one of the most beloved boats ever to sail this body of water. Years later Elias Harris who for a time was her master wrote of her: "This boat was one of the finest and fastest steamers of her day...and admired by steamboatmen as well as all others!" Aside from the new ample deck areas the Minne had a salon which was the epitome of graciousness. She was however to know some lean years.

The steamboat company soon received another staggering blow to their wobbly financial status. The Civil War broke out reducing tourist traffic to a minimum as the nation's heart was torn in half. The company cut expenses where possible. It even abolished the office of captain, a most extraordinary step! The Minne operated in charge of her engineer assisted by a pilot and clerk. Apparently this cutback didn't work out too well, for the following season the captaincy was given Elias Harris, his first command on the lake. Perhaps by then he'd grown the long beard he wore on surviving photographs of him since it would add dignity although the master's cap often sat at a rakish angle to the back of his head.

Business picked up when the war ended. The Minne steamed proudly along with full complements of passengers, among whom one day, was General George McCellan of the Army of the Potomac. However the company's board had had enough. They sold the Minne with a sigh of relief to The Champlain Transportation Company which had long operated the sidewheelers on the larger lake. Eventually this company in turn came under the control of the D&H Railroad which by 1882 had spur lines running to both ends of Lake George. Boat and train schedules were coordinated. Local citizens both at Caldwell and Ticonderoga celebrated the new spur lines with parades and fanfare as a great boon to the area. Both lines have been discontinued today.

Posters of that day announced the best means of travel northward to the lake country as follows. Hudson River night boats left their piers at the foot of Canal Street, New York City at 6PM arriving at Troy or Albany next morning. The traveller then went by rail to Moreau Station below Glens Falls where a transfer was made "to a line of fast stagecoaches which pass through Glens Falls". The stages continued "up the plank", a term which referred to the frequent necessity of corduroying the road where it crossed sand or mud. Logs or planks were laid transversly in such spots producing a surface much like the material of the same name and not exactly comfortable riding! The next stop was at the toll gate at Brown's Halfway House. While toll was collected here dusty throats could collect their own reward. From all accounts the genial Mr. Brown served excellent "lemonade", both with and without lemons! Then with a flourish the stage rolled on under the tollgate. Mr. Stoddard wrote in his famous guidebook "... as bows the stately goose to enter a sixteen foot barn door so ducked we as we passed under that tollgate!" The gate stood at the present junction of routes 9 and 149.

The stage arrived at Caldwell at mid-day. Travellers read notices that the steamer Minne-Ha-Ha would leave her dock at the fashionable Ft. Wm. Henry Hotel mornings at 7:30, Sundays excepted, returning at 6 PM.

In 1867, due to the rise in tourist traffic, the steamboat company built a second boat to take the run from the northern end of the lake and return. Travel was lighter on this schedule consequently the steamer could be smaller and screw propelled. Paddlewheelers have a shallower draft   and   they can be wider affording more deck space, large salons and cabins. Propellar driven boats must be of deeper draft and narrower. Thus the sidewheelers could still land near shore while being infinitely more spacious. They were essential on the more popular runs since a propeller boat of like size simply couldn't land at most lake points.

The Ganouskie.

The small steamer was named "Ganouskie" which was an Indian name for the deep bay north of Bolton now called Northwest Bay. She had the perky aspect of many a stubby character with a pilot house and tiny cabin on her upper deck. Her jolly skipper was not small! His name was Arnold Hulett, a man who loved to mingle with his passengers and give forth of his knowledge of the lake, both fact and yarnery. He would proudly assert that "there's not a rock or reef in the waters of Lake George that I don't know!" Once while making this comforting statement the Ganouskie struck a rock! Fortunately she scraped over it unharmed while the jovial skipper continued blandly: "Why, there's one of them now!" Hulett frequently was observed piloting the Ganouskie with his anything but dainty feet on the spokes of the wheel while perched atop a high stool, the rest of his bulk leaning comfortably against the wall.

Travellers from the north now found the Ganouskie awaiting them near the lake's outlet each morning. Prior to 1875 the passengers arrived by stagecoach which brought them from Lake Champlain via the village of Ticonderoga. In '75 that spur line of the D&H Railroad was completed between the lakes. By then Ticonderoga had begun to realize its enormous heritage of history as being of interest to travellers. Part of that heritage lay torn down and crumbling on a promontory overlooking Champlain, part lay in the strange tale of Major Duncan Campbell and the ghost who had warned him of an oddly named place before he came to America and part lay with the bones of young Lord Howe whose men would have followed him to hell and back again had he lived! It lay in the cool courage of the French general Montcalm and his men who defended Carillon against a vastly greater army and won. It lay too in the words "Surrender in the name of the Great Jehovah and the Continental Congress", and in the fiery leadership of a man named Benedict Arnold whose tragedy was played out later down on the Hudson!

1867

The Northern Tour of the lakes was becoming ever more popular. Business was good for the Minne and the Ganouskie. In 1870 they'd even gotten the mail franchise for all points along their course. Cap'ns Harris and Hulett polished up their stories some of which, fortunately, are not lost to posterity. They were recorded in the yearly guidebooks by S.R. Stoddard who doubtless enjoyed them immensely! In spite of the errant rock which dared get in the way of the little Ganouskie, Hulett, like Harris, knew the lake very well having sailed it since early boyhood. He hailed from Dresden, a tiny community east of Black Mt. Stoddard's guide of 1876 includes the following tale which was often told by the large master of the Ganouskie.

40

It was common belief then, although since proven erroneous, that Lake George contained as many islands as there are days in a year. Who started this rumor or whether lakers actually believed it I do not know, but it made an interesting talking point. The story soon made it even better! In order to keep things straight there was said to be a 366th island which appeared however only in leap years. Quite a few people met this island every fourth year when it was in the process of coming up, surfacing, or going down again. (Some still do!) Its position and description varied considerably depending on who told the story and why. Hulett vowed, "It's always getting in my way! Fact!" Another captain, Lee Harris, of the pocket-sized steamer "Owl", related as well that he'd anchored the Owl in deep water one evening only to find the boat high and dry on the cursed thing next morning. Apparently it had surfaced with unusual speed that year.

Such ingenious explanations are by no means dead. Quite recently a well known fishing guide was asked by the party he was taking out whether there were not many shoals and dangerous rocks in the lake? The guide was a man of few words, he merely nodded his head in the affirmative. After some thought he felt called upon to say; "There's one right out here called the North Shoal as a matter of fact." With that the boat lurched slightly as her keel scraped rocks. The guide re-mained calm. "Reckon that's it", he said as they proceeded on into the narrows.

In 1877 the valiant Minne was at last retired from active service, followed a few years later by the Ganouskie. They were replaced by much larger steamers, "Horicon I" in 1877 and "Ticonderoga" in 1884. It was not until 1894 that another screw propelled smaller boat was added to the line. This was "Mohican I". She was built by Captain Everett Harrison of Glens Falls who sold her to the steamboat com-pany in 1895, ostensibly for the Paradise Bay excusion run.

As for the little Ganouskie she lay idle for a number of years at the Baldwin shipyard. Then she was purchased, minus boilers and engine, by Captain G. W. Howard who had her towed to Big Burnt Island in the narrows. Moored along the shore of the island the old boat became a floating saloon. One rather curious embel-lishment of her new decor was reminiscent of Old Dick of John Jay days. A box said to have been kept on the bar contained a number of live rattlesnakes! Just what effect this may have had on customers is hard to say.

Another rare story heard along the lake some years ago is attributed to Elias Harris. He may have inherited it himself from some earlier tongue-in-cheek source. Whatever the case may be it went like this:

"Where does all the ice in the lake go in spring? Now let me tell ye, it sinks plumb to the bottom and stays there. That's often so deep down its been pilin' there for years 'cause it's mighty cold down there. Folks tell thet one spring some fishermen hooked into a big cake of it an' hauled it up. 'Twas terrible heavy and what do you think was in it? There was an' old Indian chief of some tribe all frozen stiff inside it. He was all done up in war paint and feathers too! Must be he'd got kilt or drownded in one of them wars they had around here years ago. That ice'd presarved 'im perfect all that time!" It was certainly a splendid story for young travellers to remember!

Captain Harris published his memoirs in 1903 just after his retirement, as men-tioned earlier. He wrote that it had been he who first noted the obvious shape of the mountain just south of Huletts Landing. He named it "My Elephant". It is known as Elephant Mt. today. The mountain just across the lake is called "Deer's Leap". It was named, Harris claimed, by his uncle and another hunter who had driven a great buck to his death on the mountain. Pursued by their dogs the desperate animal had leapt off a cliff to his death in the forest below. (Deer hunting with dogs is now of course illegal.)

The good captain also claimed he knew the origin of the name "Shelving Rock", the small mountain at the southeastern entrance of the narrows. According to Harris the name was first applied by hunters and lumbermen to the brook nearby. The tumbling stream could easily be crossed at a certain point by way of a shelving ledge of rock. The name was soon given the mountain. I can neither doubt nor verify this statement and probably no one living today can do so.

The story of the beloved steamer Minne-Ha-Ha, in spite of her retirement in 1877, was not yet done. She has, in fact, not entirely left the lake she served so long and faithfully. She had seen many a new resort built along the lake in her active days, including some in the beautiful narrows. Her bones rest near the forgotten ruins of one of the latter. How she came to be there is part of another chapter.

Pole rigged lamp for night fishing and other things.

Chapter 5

Mr. Smith's Island

That Erastus C. Smith was something of a character all his life there can be no doubt, but he was a pioneer in his own way too. It was he who decided to build the first hotel way down in the wild and lovely narrows of the lake and he chose an island to build it on!

The lake's islands, unless long in private ownership, cannot be bought today. They are state land. There was, however, a time during the last century when the state paid scant attention to them, did not anticipate their potential recreational value. Relatively few rugged individuals found the islands delightful campsites remote from villages and transportation facilities. Those early campers were free to choose any island and stay as long as they liked. Further, the state wasn't averse to selling some of these scattered bits of land or leasing others for the erection of private summer homes. In both instances this barred them to campers. The sale of islands was halted in 1876 but the practice of leasing continued for quite some years.

Early area guidebooks did offer suggestions to would-be campers. It was noted that the steamers would tow small boats to any point along their routes for the added fee of 50¢. The steamers could also accommodate campers by dumping cakes

Fallen giant of the woods.   Painting by the Author

of ice overboard as close to the chosen campsite as possible. This provided refrigeration for food which most generally was stored in holes in the ground covered with bark or planks. Stoddard's early guides listed as necessary items for campers an ax, fork, knife and spoon and fishing tackle. Markets were far away and fresh fish could be a welcome meal.

For those who could not bring or wish to bother with a tent a lean-to of boughs was suggested with a bed made of the same. There was then no law against the cutting of brush or trees such as later became necessary. A pillow could be made of a bag stuffed with moss or leaves. This was quite aptly looked upon as "roughing it". Prior to Smith's hotel it was the only way of making a sojourn within the remote narrows. There were a few trappers' or lumbermen's cabins along shore and that was all.

Around 1856 William Smith of Albany, Erastus' father, bought six choice islands of the state for $400! These were Dome, Clay, Crown, Turtle, Oahu and Fourteen Mile islands. Erastus inherited several of them in due course. When he decided to build a hotel on one of them, intending it at first primarily for hunters and fishermen, he chose Fourteen Mile. The attractive white pillared place opened in the late 1860s when the Minne was steaming proudly up and down the lake. Smith's choice of location was decided not only by the 12 acre size of the island but because it lay along a favorite steamboat channel, an essential factor.

The island lies at the southeastern end of the narrows close to the cliff walls of little Shelving Rock Mt. A narrow channel separates it from the mainland. The hotel and its pier were on the western side of the island. The pier is one of the few old steamer landings surviving today.

Erastus didn't run the hotel himself. He engaged R.G. Bradley and Company to do this for him which left him free to entertain his guests especially if they were young, fair and female! As young Stoddard, a contemporary, noted in his guidebook of 1873 "The Chesterfieldian owner spends his summers here and his ear is always open to the cry of beauty in distress, his boat and willing arm ready for voyages of discovery.."

One such voyage almost ended in disaster. On a warm summer day of 1870 Smith, his sister Julia, and several guests set out in a rowboat to find a pleasant picnic spot. A severe storm blew up suddenly, as is often possible on this lake. By nightfall the wind and rain had not diminished and the boat had not returned. Guests and employees of the hotel got out lanterns and waved them on the southern point of the island hoping to guide the little boat to safety. There was no sign of it and concern deepened. There was great relief next morning when the wanderers arrived unharmed, They had spent a hungry, uncomfortable, but safe night on a rocky spine of an island which Smith forthwith christened "Refuge". The island bears the name today.

Soon the small hotel was enlarged to accommodate forty guests. It had proved popular with more than sportsmen! The original graceful design suffered a bit for the square-pillared porch was swallowed into a rather plain rectangular building. However the Bradleys had brought with them a lady always known simply as "Miss Jane" who'd established quite a reputation for "setting a fine table"! This is no detriment to a resort. Mr. Smith could congratulate himself on his venture and enjoy himself to boot!

One day when the hotel was young a strange looking sailboat arrived at its pier.

"Stagecoach baggage tag."

The sail bore a curious "coat of arms" depicting a tall thin man astride a camera in pursuit of a winged money bag! The skipper himself has described his arrival by imagining a conversation between "E.C." (Smith) and a guest named Jack:

E.C.! See that boat coming out there?"

Jack, "I'm looking at it. Elegant thing isnt it? Looks like a snow plow with a dry goods box on the hind end."

E.C. "Exactly,.....sails like a stone boat...and will go every way but straight ahead. Know that long fellow lying around loose on the box trying to steer?...Well that's Stoddard the photographer and that's his boat "The Wanderer". He wanders around all over the lake taking views and money...Well there he comes, apparatus and all, to lead us to temptation".

Jack "Where's he from?"

E.C. "Glens Falls, a pretty little village but getting to be rather a tough place now!"

Smith did indeed grumble at the price of photographs of his island resort but he was quite ready to have the place described in Stoddard's guidebooks!

Seneca Ray Stoddard was born in 1844 (43?) on a farm in Saratoga County. He left home, not being farm-minded, at the age of sixteen and supported himself by versatility and talent in the artistic field. He did such work as painting decorations on the insides of railroad cars and stagecoaches. Then he discovered the possibilities inherent in a camera and set up a photographic studio in Glens Falls. Through his subsequent lifetime he produced a record of his times in photographs which remains remarkable today. He also began to write guidebooks which eventually far exceeded this area in their scope, for his travels took him as far as Alaska on this continent and east across the sea to the Holy Land. His photos and books have left us pictures both verbal and visual not only of places but of the people who drove stages, guided, operated steamboats and railroads, were hotel hosts and guests; in short worked, played and travelled in the latter half of the 19th century. In fact he continued his work almost until his death in 1917. Among his most famous illustrated lectures were those on the Adirondacks with which mountains his name is indelibly linked. It is less well known that this man was very instrumental in persuading the state legislature to establish the Adirondack Park.

It is evident that Stoddard was endowed with an irrepressible sense of humor. It runs through his writings like the bubbling exuberance of the mountain streams he loved. Here is his description of a stagecoach journey with his brother-in-law from his Adirondack Guide of 1875:

"We couldn't get knocked out (of the coach) for the sides were buttoned down and the roof firm...for we tried it. Sometimes the professor's side would rise up and he would start for me...when his side went down I would sail majestically over and light on him. Sometimes the vehicle would jump over a log, and we, rising like young eagles would soar toward the roof...Then it would go down into deep holes and stop in such a decided sort of way that we would feel our heads expecting to find our backbones sticking through our hats!" This was undoubtedly a good description of many a stagecoach ride through the mountains!

The Fourteen Mile Island House soon had evenings of dancing or music at which its owner began to have a bit of competition as regarded the fairer guests! The hotel was invaded and enlivened by a group of young men from Glens Falls who called themselves "The Waltonians". This club, first formed in 1853, had earlier occupied an island near Hague still called Waltonian Island. In 1870 fire ravaged the island so the club betook itself to Phelps (now Mohican) Island which lies just across the narrows from Fourteen Mile. The luxury of their camp became almost legendary, the members even designing for themselves a sort of uniform!

Again here are Stoddard's words: "The Waltonians had come in all the glory of their new uniforms and ordinary mortals were at a discount among the feminine portion of guests at Fourteen Mile Island. Young men wandered disconsolately about and cast ominous glances toward the camp on Phelps Island. Even the velvet coat and embroidered slippers . . . were entirely overlooked for the more recent importation of gray frocks and white military caps. Indignation meetings were held...the question of spring guns and bear traps was mooted, but to no avail. The Waltonians had the inside track, and kept it!"

Invitations to dine at the "canvas establishment" were eagerly sought and in return young ladies at the hotel gave evening receptions in the hotel parlor, with Mr. Smith at the piano! Stoddard added: "...while intoxicating music rose and fell...the old codgers who had come for a quiet time stumped grimly about the island swearing...until their venerable noses grew red with wiping and their hoary locks were damp with the dews of midnight!" This last quote suggests strongly that Mr. Stoddard himself had some good times on the island and that Erastus Smith with competition at hand didn't give up easily! Erastus, however, never married.

By 1876 two more hotels had opened on the eastern shore of the narrows close to Fourteen Mile Island. Their stories are told in succeeding chapters. Mr. Smith's hotel had lost its uniqueness of location as well as R.G. Bradley and the redoubtable

"Miss Jane set 'a fine table.' "

Miss Jane. Whatever the reason, "E.C." decided to sell both Fourteen Mile and Oahu islands retaining only Turtle. Both islands were bought by General Peter Bellinger of New Jersey who continued to operate the resort while building himself a cottage on Oahu. After a time he too decided to sell Fourteen Mile and its hotel.

For some time the Steamboat Company had been looking for a likely place mid-lake where excursionists riding the steamers could disembark for several hours to picnic and swim. The need for such a spot was apparent to the company in order to keep in the good graces of hotels they served. Many social groups were finding the lake cruise a nice one-day outing but had taken to going ashore for a time at some resort landing. The hotels were not enthusiastic about picnickers on their lawns. General Bellinger however declined the company's offer for Fourteen Mile Island, unwilling to see the island overrun, its natural beauty jeopardized.

One day an elderly man came to stay at the island hotel. He puttered around and got to know Bellinger quite well. Surprisingly he came up with an offer for the place which the General accepted. He found out too late that his erstwhile guest was a front man for the steamboat company but the deed was done and the company took title to the island for $15,000. in 1888. It began happily running excursions there, leasing the old hotel to one Hannibal Allen. The General could only retire to his summer home on Oahu to brood.

Stoddard kept pace with events. Of Fourteen Mile Island he now wrote: "On the east separating it from the mainland, is a narrow and deep channel through which the largest steamers can pass. Here is another dock where excusion steamers land. This east side has been fitted up...for picnic parties, with refreshment rooms, a dancing pavilion, croquet grounds, swings, photographic gallery, etc." The narrow channel became known as Lovers' Lane!

It was after an evening run from Baldwin to the island and return that a fire smouldered unnoticed under the boiler room on the steamer "Ticonderoga" (This boat is not to be confused with the one on Champlain nor the present one of that name on this lake.) When she started on her regular run next morning the fire fanned by her forward motion, soon engulfed her. No one was hurt, fortunately. The year was 1901.

By the early 1900s the popularity of excursions to the island had waned and the Steamboat Company in turn decided to sell. In 1905 the island was bought as a private summer place by W. Beardsley, president of the Florida East Coast Railroad. His family lived in the old hotel until the large home on the southern end of the island was completed. Then Mr. Smith's hotel ceased to exist. The island is still privately owned.

As for Erastus Corning Smith himself, he'd gone to live on his last remaining island. This was Turtle, of no mean size. His house was known as "Green Oakes". E.C. spent the last active summers of his life there becoming known all along the lake as "Old 'Rastus" and as quite a character! He no longer used a boat, but relied on friend or stranger to take him wherever he wanted to go. Lonely perhaps, he would sight a boat and run along the shore of his island waving and shouting until some kindly soul stopped and took him aboard. Even then there was enough of the gallant left in him to recite Shakespearian sonnets to fair fellow passengers!

Old Rastus died in the Griffin farmhouse in North Bolton almost directly opposite and in sight of the island on which so many years earlier he had built his hotel. Thereafter Turtle Island was re-sold to the state.

1757 British sloop destroyed by French troops at head of Lake George near Ft. William Henry. It was raised from bottom in 1903 and later cut up for souvenirs!   *Photo by A.N. Thompson*

Stage for Lake George at Glens Falls Railroad Station   *Stoddard Photo*

50

Stage at Halfway House Tollgate now junction of Routes 9 and 149.   *Stoddard Photo*

Stage leaving Ft. William Henry Hotel [*second*]   *Stoddard Photo*

Enormous second Fort William Henry Hotel at the head of lake. Steamer Ganouskie at pier.   *Stoddard Photo*

Steamers Minne-Ha-Ha and Ganouskie at Caldwell

A cable railroad was built and operated to top of Prospect Mt., Caldwell.

Little charter steamer "Owl." Her skipper also found the 366th island   *Stoddard Photo*

Ganouskie at Wilson House pier, Bolton Landing   *Stoddard Photo*

The Ganouskie heads toward the narrows. Note "lonely little clearing" of mill at Shelving Rock Falls in distance.

Stoddard Photo

Sagamore Hotel, Bolton Landing, burned in 1914   *Stoddard Photo*

Winter aerial view northward over Northwest Bay and the narrows.   *Photo by Richard Dean*

Ganouskie landing at E.C. Smith's Fourteen Mile Island House.   *Stoddard Photo*

Original Fourteen Mile Island House. *Stoddard Photo*

Fourteen Mile Island House after enlargement. *Stoddard Photo*

Self portrait, Seneca Ray Stoddard.

Fourteen Mile Island Hotel from north.

Stoddard Photo

A-fishin' or a-courtin'? Fourteen Mile Island.   *Stoddard Photo*

Steamer Ticonderoga I, 1884-1901.   *Stoddard Photo*

The "Ti" landing at Bolton.
Stoddard Photo

The "Ti" burns in 1901.
Press Photo

Mohican I, Fourteen Mile Island and Shelving Rock.   *Stoddard Photo*

First railroad station of the D & H Caldwell · 1882.

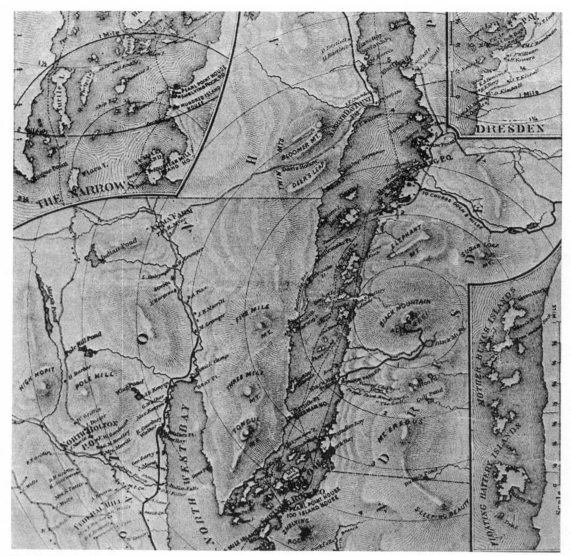

Map by S.R. Stoddard

Chapter 6

R. G. Bradley and Company and Shelving Rock

It's very likely that during the summer of 1874 Erastus Smith spent some thoughtful moments in the little gazebo which stood on the northern end of Fourteen Mile Island. Things were happening at the foot of Shelving Rock Mt. a scant half mile away. Reuben Bradley, Smith's factotum at the Fourteen Mile Island Hotel, had left Smith's employ, acquired land over there and was building a hotel of his own on it. In spite of the fact that vacationers tended to root themselves at a place if they liked it, and Smith's hotel was popular, there was another disquieting fact. Miss Jane who "set a fine table" was part of the Bradley entourage and had left with them. Good food at a resort was and is important, perhaps especially in those days when there was no choice of another eating place nearby.

Bradley opened his hotel in 1875, naming it The Hundred Island House after the nearest island group. As the Minne and Ganouskie entered the narrows from the the south there were now two hotel piers awaiting them.

Young Stoddard, by then quite established in his chosen field, soon inspected the new place. His guidebook had nice words to say about it. "It", he wrote, "has a degree of finish seldom seen in a place intended solely for summer occupancy!" He added that the building "is surmounted by a sightly observatory from which the roof may be gained (with) a view that has hardly its equal along the lake. Terms $10 to $14 a week". A Mansard roof crowned the building with elegance.

The Bradleys owned a sizable piece of land, part of it lovely lakeshore. Winding through it came the lumbermen's road from Hogtown which reached the lakeshore near the hotel to take itself on northward in sinuous fashion to a lumber camp at the foot of Black Mt. Abetted by local lumber roads and the so-called "Dacy road" plus a few trails cut by the Bradleys up and around Shelving Rock there were walks aplenty. Undoubtedly these whetted appetites for Miss Jane's culinary artistry. They also may have counteracted the adverse effects of too many delicious vittles.

In 1876 the Bradleys acquired a neighbor a few hundred yards to the north. The Pearl Point House was built there on a very beautiful thumb of land. Its story follows later. It was however the Hundred Island House and its acreage which about two decades later became the nucleus of the largest private estate in the eastern Adirondacks. In the early days of the Shelving Rock hotels the surrounding slopes bore clear witness to recent lumbering. The so-called second growth was small, the rocky ledges showed clearly. During the days of the estate which succeeded them the forest was carefully allowed to regain maturity, the region was never lumbered again.

The Hundred Island House like all others of the time had a needed complement of service buildings not required by a resort after the advent of electricity. Aside from a stable and laundry there was the equally indispensible ice-house. Wherever people lived there was need of ice for refrigeration. All cities, villages and country places depended on frozen rivers, lakes and ponds where ice harvesting formed a great winter business, providing work for scores of men. When

the ice had frozen to a proper thickness it was marked out and sawed into huge blocks. These were loaded onto horse-drawn sleighs which hauled them ashore to the icehouses. It of course behooved resorts to have their own buildings, as it did farmers and cottagers or other residents of more isolated places. The buildings were tall, windowless structures with massive doors beside which, on the outer wall, ladders were usually nailed. The ice blocks were laid down tier on tier inside with sawdust between each layer. Since they were packed almost to the roof the iceman had a long climg up the ladder early in the season. He went armed with a shovel, ax, enormous iron tongs, and a fair amount of muscle. The old fashioned wooden ice boxes devoured ice in hot weather so the supply had to be ample!

Other provisions also had to be made for the comfort of guests, which required elbow grease. Wood was needed both for heat and cooking. Large woodsheds had to be filled with wood of varying lengths, some split for easy kindling. Axes, saws and wedges had to be kept sharp and ready.

My questions about the old ways were in many cases answered by one who knew very well what he was talking about. His name is John Stiles. John came to work as a very young man early in the present century on the large estate mentioned above. The era of the narrows hotels were just ending, old ways had barely begun to change.

John was employed on the estate for some fifty years thereafter, in time becoming overseer of its 7600 odd acres. No more recent picture of the Shelving Rock narrows area could be complete without the presence of his wiry figure somewhere in it. A woodsman born, John like others of his kind has always seemed to have a rapport with nature plus a sort of joy in a contest with the elements be it on land or water. No storm, ice, heat, or howling gale will stop this sort when he sets out to do whatever he has a mind to do. Small wonder "Gentleman Johnny" Burgoyne was halted at Saratoga in 1777. He had encountered another generation of the same sort.

John acquired his knowledge of woods, fields, brooks, and lake and all that abounds therein as most good woodsmen do, through ears, eyes, nose, and that almost indefinable but indispensable quality called instinct. (If ye know where a thing should be it most generally is . . . if a certain critter had oughtta be just over the rise he's most often there.) John passed such knowledge on in his own gentle soft spoken way to several generations of children who spent at least part of each year at Shelving Rock, myself included. He knew the language of the forest, the habits of its inhabitants, plant, bird, beast and fish. Nor was he, incidentally, often fooled by homo sapiens!

Sometimes we'd find him growling and stroking the stock of his gun. The imps with the ringed tails had gotten to his corn just as it ripened or perhaps the sharp hooved ones had pawed up beets and carrots after they'd finished off the tops. But he knew how we felt and if open warfare ever resulted he shielded us from the knowledge. Anyway that's for him to say.

John's step is a mite slower now, of course, less springy, but he still talks of deer and people, fish, horses and ice cracks, boats, bears and bobcats, Lucinda's mighty burnin' spells, all "by Judas, in them day when things was mighty different!"

Of course John has his own fund of tall stories! He's always claimed that over South Bay way where he was born and raised, folks grew some mighty pumpkins and squash! Their seeds were so big that people used them as shingles on their houses. "Sure thing!"

Since many questions came to mind about the old days and ways, how this or that necessity was provided, I went to John for some answers.

"John, the Hundred Island House sat a ways back from shore and there's no brook there. How did they get lake water to the building?"

"Why hecky," he said, "first off them Bradleys as owned it kept a special horse walkin' a treadmill 'n that pumped water up to a tank on Shelving Rock. Then of course t'was gravity feed. Later they got a steam pump. 'Course in them days there warn't no rooms with runnin' water, bath n' all." His eyes twinkled. "Folks had to go down the hall apiece cause water was piped only to parts of the buildin'."

"Kerosene lights I 'spose?"

"Sure. Your grandpa had 'em at your cottage when you was little remember?" I nodded remembering very well what happened if some one came in a door at night from windward! The lamp chimneys would blacken in a flash!

"T'was quite a job at them old hotels, trimmin' wicks, cleanin' chimneys 'n fillin' 'em every day! After a time they got that acetylene gas a man had to make, first off, so to speak. He'd drop pellets of carbide into a tank (water) 'n that formed the gas. Later t'was done automatic."

The Bradleys' venture was well endowed it would seem. They had a patient horse, plenty of available wood and ice, and last but not least the marvelous Miss Jane whose last name, for the curious, was Rourke. The hotel became a social center for nearby cottagers and campers, its steamboat pier was the landing for most of them, it was also the post office. By this time people were beginning to lease an island of the state for erection of a summer bungalow. The practice would continue for some years until the state began to think twice about it, as will be seen later. Meanwhile such cottage owners could dine, dance and attend other functions at the hotels. Country clubs were things of the future.

For almost two decades the Bradleys ran their hotel. Somewhere around 1890 things began to go a little badly. Rube Bradley was no longer young but his daughters and the redoubtable Miss Jane strove valiantly to meet mounting debts. The place needed renovating. Then in 1893 a tragedy occurred involving the hotel but in no way the fault of its owners. Local conjecture has always claimed however that this spelled the end for R.G. Bradley and Co. and conjecture often contains more than a grain of truth.

On a stormy August night in 1893, the Hundred Island House was holding its weekly hop, a dance at which guests of other hotels, cottagers and campers were welcome. Twenty three guests of the hotel on Fourteen Mile Island (then no longer owned by E.C. Smith) decided to attend. That stormy night rowboats were out of the question even for the short crossing. Instead an envoy went to the Pearl Point Hotel to request the rental of a small steamboat berthed there. The manager demurred since the boat's captain was absent but finally agreed to let a young employee and the regular engineer make the brief trip. Once aboard ladies took shelter in the small cabin. In the wild wind and coming darkness the pilot miscalculated. The boat struck the remains of an old pier off the mainland but her forward speed caused her to careen over it into deeper water. The boat's hull had been ripped wide open, there was time only for one frantic distress whistle. The little steamer, "The Rachael," sank within three minutes in twenty feet of water taking eight women and one man down with her.

That whistle was heard at the Hundred Island House. Guests and employees streamed outdoors, every available lantern was collected as men shed shoes and coats for rescue efforts. They set out in rowboats, the lanterns smoking and flickering in the wild night. The hotel's kindly housekeeper had blankets and beds ready as terrified survivors were brought ashore. It was soon evident that some had not been so lucky. Their bodies were recovered next day and found temporary resting places on the hotel's billiard tables. Newpapers far and wide carried headlines of the tragedy.

Many horrified guests of the Hundred Island House hurriedly packed and left.

Nor did they speak of returning next season. It may well have been the final blow for the Bradleys. By 1894 there was no alternative, hotel and land were to be sold at public auction.

The day of the auction arrived with auctioneers and bidders milling around the grounds. Witnessed by only a few, a small privately rented steamboat put in at the pier. Aboard was a Chicago couple, a gentleman and his second wife who were touring the lake on their honeymoon. Struck by the beauty of the area the gentleman wasted no time. He made an outright offer for the entire property, hotel and land. It was promptly accepted and the auction never took place. The new owner was George O. Knapp co-founder of the Union Carbide Corporation.

Mr. Knapp promptly engaged the former manager of the Lake House at Caldwell, Henry Nichols, to run the hotel. The building itself was extensively renovated and the Knapp family spent summers there. Among other things a trout pond was built and stocked a short distance to the south and a gigantic water toboggan shot sporting guests into the lake with a mighty splash. Rooms could now be had "en suite with private bath." Call bells and fire alarms added to the comfort and security. Decorative shrubs and trees were planted on the grounds which at night were lighted by electricity! This was generated in a little power house at the mouth of Shelving Rock Brook a mile or so away. A steam yacht "Vanadis" and a steam launch "Kismet" were available along with a handsome fleet of cedar and mahogany rowboats. The Adirondack skiff has a place in history all its own but many a fine rowboat was built by skilled craftsmen throughout the mountains. One of the master builders on Lake George was Fred Smith Sr. of Bolton Landing who continued to make them until about 1930. Such boats can be classed as collectors' items today, their construction, unfortunately, almost a lost art.

The Hundred Island House even acquired a telegraph wire. It looped its way from tree to tree up several miles of very rugged shoreline to the south with only the trace of a maintenance trail below. The brochure which mentions it proudly also tells of facilities for quoits, lawn tennis, archery and croquet along with what it terms "row-sail boats with patent folding center boards". The booklet adds that "numerous roads and bridle paths are being constructed including one to Black Mt. Point to the north". The latter followed much the course of the old lumbermen's road but was often carried closer to the lakeshore by stone retaining walls. Anyone who walks it today will see traces of the older road but most of the skidways and tote roads off the mountains have disappeared. Trails were cut up and around Shelving Rock and a thirty foot observation tower placed on the summit. Along the main climb, rest and panoramic views could be had at three rustic summerhouses. The second was a real cliff-hanger and will be remembered by some for it survived until quite recently. It perched like an eagle's aerie atop the northern cliff face of the mountain. For many years it held an acetylene lantern that was a welcome beacon to navigators in the area. For a time it was a custom to light part of the trail with a string of "Magic Fire" each Fourth of July. To quote John Stiles, "T'was quite a sight, all them colored flames strung out like a chain across the slope!"

The trail around Shelving Rock was proof that Longfellow's Hiawatha was still a popular source of names. It was known as The Nennemoosha (Sweetheart) Spring Trail in fine romantic style. The trail exists today only for those who remember its course but the brochure described the "crystal clear spring where a summer house

has been built" along its deeply forested upper reaches. The cold clear spring still bubbles out in its hidden place. The remarkable switch-backing road which forms part of today's state hiking trail up the mountain, crossing the older trail, was built some years later as a carriage road for Mr. Knapp. Its difficult construction was the work of Jack Dacy assisted by Herman Benton, brother of Lucinda White.

Jack Dacy's fine broad farm acres lay in the higher country behind Shelving Rock and just below the bold rocky chin of Sleeping Beauty Mountain. Years earlier his father had come there, built a home and cleared the land. No vestiges of that house or its barns and outbuildings remain for Jack subsequently built a house of his own nearby. The foundations of this house and its barns are still very visible since it stood until the state acquired the land from the Knapp Estate in 1941. The massive mountain rising almost sheerly above the site towers over little Shelving Rock down on the lakeshore as an adult towers over a child. For many years farms such as Dacy's provided lakeshore establishments with milk, cream, potatoes and other produce. Wagons loaded with those great forty quart milk cans lumbered down the four or five miles of steep mountain road almost daily. Dacy's wagon used the old "Dacy Road", now a hiking tail.

Each held about 40 quarts.

So well known was the Dacy Farm that Sleeping Beauty Mt. was locally called "Jack's Pinnacle"! Little Shelving Rock was off-handedly spoken of as "The Cobble". That large upland farm was perhaps best known for the fine white potatoes it produced. Many folks crossed the lake to buy them off the wagon which was driven to Log Bay where they could land with their boats.

Dacy was a man of enormous strength. He wouldn't hire a farm hand who couldn't equal his own feats! The man had to be able to uproot a small tree and lift a barrel of potatoes onto a wagon by himself. The barrels weighted upwards of 150 lbs.

The following story is still told around the countryside. One day when Dacy was a young lad of sixteen he heard a great commotion down in his father's sheep fold. Running out to see what was causing it he found two bear cubs inside. One cub promptly headed off for the woods but the other took refuge in a tree. Turning, the lad saw the mother bear charging straight at him in defense of her young. Young

Shelving Rock Falls

Dacy got to another tree in a mighty hurry and scaled it but repeatedly had to swing by his arms from a branch in order to kick the enraged bear in the head as she clawed up the tree after him! Only womenfolk were at home, they heard the boy's shouts but having no weapons rushed off to the neighbors for help. In the meanwhile the cub, seeing mother on the job, descended his tree and went off. His parent followed, fortunately. A thoroughly frightened boy climbed down at last. On the way home he met a strange sight! The neighbors had responded quickly and came marching through the fields armed with whatever weapons had been most handy. They carried crowbars, rakes, clubs, pitchforks and one gun. For years afterwards folks who came to visit the Dacys had to see the tree whose lower bark still hung in shreds from the bear's claws!

The Dacy farm eventually became part of the Knapp Estate but is now state land. On selling the place Jack Dacy moved to Ft. Ann village where he lived until his death.

In the early 1900s Mr. Knapp selected a site for a large summer home for himself and his family. Meanwhile the estate was increasing in size yearly, some of it quickly acquired when lumber interests again threatened to denude lakeshore and mountains. The site chosen for the house was some 200 feet up on the slope of Shelving Rock. Actually it was the location of the lowest of the little gazebos on the mountain trail, a place from which views to south, west and north over the island studded narrows were superb. However the first architect taken to see the proposed site shook his head. He declared flatly, "Impossible!" To him the steepness of the slope precluded any thought of a large home there. Verticle ledges rose above while the ground sloped only a little less steeply downward to the lakeshore. An architect was finally found who would undertake the job but first he had to construct high and massive walls of stone to hold the building. The house itself was built of wood. It was completed in 1902. A few years later the old hotel below was torn down.

The Hundred Island House land and many added acres now became a private estate but the roads and trails which ran unobtrusively through it were never closed to anyone who wished to enjoy them. As mentioned elsewhere the property finally came to encompass some eight miles of narrows shoreline, Black, Erebus and Sleeping Beauty Mountains and some lovely ponds which lie behind them. The forests returned to their natural growth cycles undisturbed. Henry Nichols, last manager of the hotel, became the first overseer of the entire estate.

Below the great retaining walls of the new home a rather formal garden was literally cut out of the ledges, its background the native birches, cedars, evergreens and fern and moss covered rock of the mountain. A young man was engaged to tend this garden. He'd been working at a Glens Falls greenhouse, his name, John Stiles. John's large hands had a way with plants even then!

The great walls of the house and its terraces were topped with enormous, finely cut blocks of native granite. The same huge stones were used to build the garden pool, its benches and winding sets of stairs down the ledges from above. The granite was actually quarried on the estate on one of the most beautiful points in the narrows a half mile or so south of Red Rock Bay. The stone cutters' drill marks can still be seen in ledges which slope smoothly down into the water of the lake several hundred feet below. A few carefully cut but unused blocks have remained there, by now deeply embedded in unusually thick moss. They somehow resemble a sort of

Pergola in garden on Shelving Rock

Stonehenge whose final alignment was not completed. Others were left stacked like pages of a half opened book on the old road above the point awaiting men, horses and stoneboats as had their companions.

Down on the lakeshore where the ledge slips so easily into the water there are marks far older than the stone cutters. They can clearly be seen beyond the outposts of evergreens, mosses and lichens. These are striation marks cut by the great glaciers of the ice ages.

Aside from the carriage road which wound up from the lakeshore to the house there was an electrically operated cable railway from the boathouse directly into the basement of the home. It ran straight up the slope entering the massive walls through a large archway. The railway had two miniature cars, one for passengers, another for freight.

There is one great enemy of all such rather isolated places. It is fire. During the small hours of a night in the summer of 1917 a short circuit occurred within the house in the mechanism of the little railway. The acrid smoke was not discovered until the resulting fire had made too great a headway. There was not enough water available for such a blaze. As the Knapp steam yacht "Sayonara" frantically whistled for help people came from far and near but could do no more than chop down nearby trees to prevent a forest fire. By morning the flames shot upward as wall after wall caved in. By noon only the massive stone retaining walls and tall chimneys remained. Furthermore orders were given that no one risk entering the burning building to save any of the contents. The house was a total loss and was never rebuilt. The large foundations are often a mystery to people who climb the mountain today for although the site still belongs to the Knapp family as does the land around it access to the mountail trail has never been barred.

In 1941 the bulk of the large property was sold at a very minimal price to the State of New York to remain wild forest land. However during the days that it was an estate there were quite a few people employed there, at one time they numbered about eighty. When farms such as Dacy's became part of the property they frunished homes for those employed the year round. The farmland continued to furnish food as it had for several generations. One of the old farmhouses housed a one room school, the teacher arriving in fall to live with the family in residence. The pupils, all grown men and women now, tell of going to school on snowshoes when drifts were too deep along the mountain roads. Some rode to school on the mules Mr. Knapp kept for packing into the mountains.

While the pupils solved their problems as to how to get to school, their fathers often crossed the frozen lake for mail and supplies since this was on the whole easier than tackling the snow choked road to Ft. Ann. Road plowing was not quite what it is today. For crossings on the ice the men always carried planks to bridge possible ice cracks. John Stiles will casually relate that the main difficulty, whatever the vehicle if one was used, was to get the front wheels on those planks. "After that t'was easy!" Cracks can widen, shift or become ridges very quickly at times but these were the odds they took their chances on for the return trip. It is also true that a snowstorm on the lake is as impenetrable as dense fog, a sense of direction can be easily lost while there's always the danger of wandering onto thin ice.

When horses were still in use on such expeditions they were shod with calked shoes to prevent sliding and slipping. Men sometimes went through the ice and so

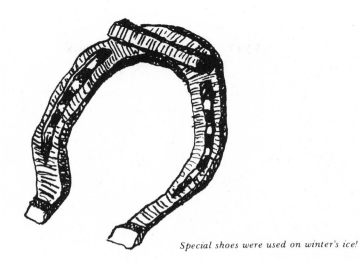

Special shoes were used on winter's ice!

did horses. (Today the cold bath can be taken in a car or snowmobile!) I've often heard John solemnly ask;

"Know what we did when a horse went through the ice? We'd git a rope 'round his neck 'n choke 'im a bit. He'd be breathin' in an' so he'd bob up an' float an' we could haul 'im out easy! Didn't harm him none either."

He'll often add this sage bit of advice. "'N if you git in yourself, git to where you fell in, that ice 'd held you to there. Take off anythin', scarf, cap, mittins, 'n lay 'em on the ice. They'll freeze down quick 'n give you somethin' to hang on to to pull yourself out."

After such talk his blue eyes will light up and look off into the distance and you know they're looking back through the years. Most generally he adds slowly:

"Judas mighty, you know somethin'? Things was mighty different in them days!"

R.G. Bradley's Hundred Island Hotel from steamer pier. *Stoddard Photo*

Archery at the Hundred Island House. *Stoddard Photo*

South over grounds of Hundred Island House. In distance on left "Lover's Lane," right old pier on whose remains the Rachael was wrecked in 1893.   *Stoddard Photo*

Hundred Island House after renovations made when purchased by George O. Knapp.   *Photo by Thatcher*

Pearl Point left, Hundred Island House center, long water toboggan on right.   *Stoddard Photo*

Shelving Rock hotels from Shelving Rock Mountain.   *Stoddard Photo*

Knapp boathouse and yacht "Sayonara," home on mountain above, also
gazebo top of cliff.
Photo Courtesy of Mrs. Jesse Stiles

Northward over the narrows from site of Knapp home.   Photo by William Steinback

Stables and carriage house on Knapp Estate.   *Photo Courtesy of Mrs. Jesse Stiles*

George O. Knapp home on Shelving Rock [burned 1917].   *Photo Courtesy of Mr. and Mrs. G. Owen Knapp*

The garden on Shelving Rock. *Photo Courtesy of Mrs. Jesse Stiles*

Cable railway emerging from the Knapp home.
Photo Courtesy of Mr. and Mrs. G. Owen Knapp

Tiny cable railroad station on lakeshore below Knapp home.

Shelving-Rock Falls.

*1872 drawing of Shelving Rock Falls show-
ing old log mill dam — from "Picturesque
America" [published 1872].*

Shelving Rock Falls.

Gorge below the falls. — Photo Courtesy of the late Walter Kenworthy once youthful assistant of Stoddard.

Above the falls.

Photo by Walter Kenworthy

Picnic at Edgemere in Lovers' Lane. Note team of oxen. [Now the home of Rev. and Mrs. Ernest Stires.]
Photo Courtesy Mrs. Jesse Stiles

Jack Dacy's farmhouse and Sleeping Beauty Mountain.   *Photo Courtesy of Mr. George R. Simon*

Dacy Farm from foot of Mountain.   *Photo Courtesy of Mr. George R. Simon*

Another view of Dacy Farm showing log watering trough.   *Photo Courtesy of Mr. George R. Simon*

Chapter 7

Islands and People

Lake George's islands number about 172. In spite of old time captains, guides, and even Mr. Stoddard who liked a good story as well as the others, there is not an island for each day of the year. Of course there are many rocky protrusions not dignified by the name island and not included in the count. Many of those rocks are miniature islands, supporting a lone scrub tree or other inveterate greenery with fortitude and clever roots. But these play host generally speaking only to birds and transient animals, not to humans. Then there's that curious island which surfaces only in leap years. Its description and location seem to have varied considerably through the years, as is still the case.

Many have loved and love the lake's islands. An island can be a small kingdom. This was certainly true for two of General Bellinger's daughters who along with a brother inherited Oahu Island. They summered there until both were well into their eighties while the brother did not remain as long. The island lies just off the tip of Tongue Mt. and receives the full force of many a wind. In spite of this the sisters scorned all means of coming and going on the lake other than in their rowboat. The slender craft would be seen in the wildest weather if the two ladies had a mind to go somewhere. They seldom missed church services in Bolton. In fact their skill with oars became almost legendary. In later years one of them in fact once remarked to a concerned friend:

"We two old ladies are far safer in our rowboat than committed to the exingencies of an engine!"

Many a kind but in this case naive boatman tried to offer help at times, such as a tow. He would be told in no uncertain terms that it was not needed or desired! Old timers knew better, they waved and went on about their affairs. Often however in my own recollection something like this would happen; uninitiated boatman to someone on the Shelving Rock mainland:

"Ahoy, ashore! There's two women out in the middle of the lake in a little rowboat. It's mighty rough! Would someone watch'em or maybe fetch'em in?"

Would come the shouted answer from shore, "Was them two wearin' kinda like poke bonnets an' one rowin' an' one settin' in the stern?"

"That's right. That's them!"

"Then don't you worry none. Them's the Bellinger girls an' you kain't drown'em!"

These old fashioned poke bonnets were eminently suitable for the sisters' voyages and the fact that the style had long vanished was of no consequence to them at all.

Once a summer until their very last years on the island the two would stock up the rowboat with provisions and bedrolls and row a complete circuit of the 32 mile lake. They went up one shore and down the other and didn't return home until the circle was done. They stayed at hotels only on the stormiest nights. They certainly came to know well the lake's secrets, its hidden coves and channels, its laughter and its rages. Mountain tops too were often on their agenda for a night's stay to see sunset and sunrise from a high place. They carried along a book on most of these trips which described the plants indigenous to the north country, adding their marginal notes as to where each was found. They did not disturb them, their love for lake, forest and field gently wrapt in this preservation. It was in its way a "reverence for life", a phrase then still largely unquoted.

As might be guessed the Bellingers didn't like intruders on their island although they were always ready to help anyone in real distress. This didn't apply to wild creatures, naturally! One fall day of dense fog on the lake they heard the unmistakable sounds of Canada geese heading southward high above the greyness. Then they heard the plaintive honking of a single goose much closer. One of the sisters went out and called to the bird, "Come here my darling, come to safety and food". Suddenly the great bird sailed out of the fog to touch down nearby, narrowly missing her. Whether it had heard her and responded who can say, but it remained a guest for several days then joined another flight. Most probably it was a young bird not yet inured to the rigors of migration. A young goose would not yet have found a mate and be alone. Canada geese mate for life. When one mate cannot continue because of injury the other will remain alongside, 'til recovery or death.

There was a young lad who did chores for the Bellingers for a time. They were fond of him and very concerned when one day he was caught on the lake on his way to the island in a violent thunderstorm. They were at the shore when he pulled in: "Were you very frightened out there in the storm?"

"Well," he answered after a moments thought, "I waren't exactly afeared. But," he added, "that don't mean I ain't got FEAR!"

Miss Bellinger would relate the incident, pause and say, "How could it have been better stated?"

In the magic of a summer evening I like to think that the course of a powerful modern boat sometimes gives way today to a ghost, the ghost of a slender, beautiful rowboat the rhythm of whose oars is steady and sure.

In 1876 the state enacted a law which put an end to sale of islands. The largest one, Long Island near the lake's head, had never been state land. It was granted to its first owners by the colonial government in 1770 and was only very recently acquired by the state. Green Island, near Bolton Landing, locaton of three successive Sagamore Hotels, was once part of a large tract obtained by patent in 1794 by one Wheeler Douglas.

By 1880 the New York Legislature had begun to regard the islands in a new light, as potential vacation camping areas. A law was passed making it a misdemeanor to cut trees or brush or otherwise deface them. In 1885 they were placed in the custody of a new Forest Commission, forerunner of today's Conservation Department. Some sources say that the legislature had become more conservation minded when large cities began to realize the jeopardization of water supplies! 1885 also saw the birth of a famous clause which was later incorporated in a constitutional amendment. The latter reads as follows:

"The lands of the state now owned or hereafter acquired constituting the Forest Preserve as now fixed by law shall be forever kept as wild forest lands. They shall not be leased, sold or exchanged or taken by any corporation public or private, nor shall the timber thereon be sold, removed, or destroyed."

This is the famous "Forever Wild" clause which has often since come under fire, plans have been repeatedly made to circumvent or change it. May this never happen!

Many of the lake's islands lie in the narrows, lovely remnants of the pre-glacial mountain barrier which existed there. All but two in that area are state land. Elsewhere along the lake islands are less grouped. Most of these but not all, are also state owned. Before 1876, as noted earlier, islands could be bought from the state. Small ones such as the Canoe Islands, Recluse, Three Brothers and Hiawatha cost about $10. Larger ones as for example Clay, Dome, Crown, Oahu and Fourteen Mile sold for $50 to $100! The state's practice of leasing islands for private summer bungalows was particularly true of the Hundred Island group in the narrows, perhaps due to the pleasant hotels nearby.

As the Forest Commission became better organized and vacation camping more and more popular because of faster and easier access from urban areas the leasing of islands began to come under severe criticism. Finally a law was passed to stop it. In 1907 the weekly "Lake George Mirror" printed the ultimatum. "Must vacate all state land. All structures are to be removed at once with the exception of the few whose leases have not expired under the earlier law." The paper went on to say: "This will effect many who are located on the islands and some propose to dispute to the last court the process of ejectment!" The latter were not successful of course. The private bungalows came down or were moved to private shorefront elsewhere. Most state islands were opened to campers.

One, probably the first island cottage built in the narrows on state owned land, was on Phantom Island. It was erected in 1870 as the home of J. Henry Hill an artist who came to live there accompanied only by his dog. He wished to draw local flora and fauna undisturbed, preferring solitude. Hill became known as The Hermit of Lake George. His dislike for visitors was especially marked if they were female, a fact Stoddard noted adding that while Hill "was third in a generation of artists there was not likely to be a fourth." Some accounts claimed that the artist spent winters on the island too. Whatever the truth of this may have been the dog had no such hermit tendencies. He eventually betook himself off and didn't return. In time the isolation proved too much for the master as well. In 1877 he suffered temporary insanity, was removed from his island home and never came back. The cottage subsequently became the summer home of the son of Queensbury's famous historian Dr. A.W. Holden. After that it was occupied by the Hon. Jerome Lapham of Glens Falls who was living there and heard the frantic distress signal of the little steamer "Rachael" in 1893 and undoubtably went out to help.

Private bungalows by then dotted many nearby islands, their post office, social center and steamboat landing either Pearl Point or the Hundred Island House. Glen Island, now ranger headquarters for campers, got its name from the Glen Club which had a cottage on it. Stoddard listed this as "The Cold Water Club, composed of solid men from Glens Falls". A photographer carried on a summer business on Uncas Island while large Big Burnt Island nearby hosted not only the old Ganouskie with its rattlesnake bar but also several wild goats, origin unknown. Ranger Island was named after its cottage owner while Gem and Juanita islands had cottages as well. A little to the south on Hen and Chicken Islands Captain Delevan Bloodgood, U.S. Navy Medical Director, put up an East Indian style bungalow which survives today on privately owned lakeshore not far away. It was moved over the ice in sections one winter by subsequent owners.

A small island to the north near the Tongue Mt. shore bears the ambiguous name "As You Were Island". It acquired its curious name in this way. Years ago an old army veteran took his boat up into the narrows a-hunting deer. As he neared the little island he saw a deer browsing on it. This was unbelievable luck! The deer's presence on an island was not in itself unusual for deer often swim the lake, sometimes when pursued, sometimes for other reasons. They did and still do rest or feed on an island occasionally. To the old man this would be an easy shot. However he suddenly had an attack of 'buck fever' or his gun misfired. Stunned and angry at his miss the man yelled out the army command, "As you were!", hoping the now alarmed animal would pause long enough for a second shot. Accounts differ from there. Some say the deer splashed off into the lake and got away, others say the old hunter got his chance.

To the north lie the Dollar Islands under the steep slopes of the Tongue Mt. Range. They were supposedly the scene of an episode in "The Last of The Mohicans". Beyond them a great amphitheater of mountain looks down on Halfway Island, mid way the lake's length. Atop the towering cliffs above eagles always used to nest but now it has been some years since anyone has told of seeing them there. I remember the magnificent freedom of their soaring flight as well as the great birds' piercing screams audible on the lake below.

Along the eastern shore north of Black Mt. are islands called The Floating Battery and Mother Bunch. The latter, according to Stoddard, were named after a rock formation on one of them people fancied resembled the figure of a woman. On seeing the rock Stoddard thought a better name would have been "Grandmother Bunch"!

The name Floating Battery has a more factual derivation. In 1758 a large British army under General James Abercrombie sailed down Lake George to attack the French at Ticonderoga. Among the scores of vessels carrying men and equipment were gunboats commonly referred to as "floating batteries." One of these came to grief and sank off the island which bears the name. It's said this boat could be seen lying under water for many years.

Mid-lake near Huletts are the lovely Harbor Islands. These were sold in 1871 to a Paulist priest, Isaac Hecker for $50. They are still owned by the Paulist fathers. There's a tiny chapel on one of them while between them a boat can "thread the needle's eye". These beautiful islands witnessed one of the most savage and bloody skirmishes of the French and Indian War. A party of British were ambushed there by Indian allies of France. Those not killed outright were tortured to death, only a handful escaping. All accounts add that cannibalism was halted only by the arrival of French officers.

The best known tale connected with the lake's islands is most surely the one involving nearby Vicars Island and a certain Captain Sam Patchen. Stoddard never left this one out of his guidebooks. In 1789 Cap'n Sam had built a house on Sabbath Day Point across the lake from Huletts. That point had known a habitation of sorts since the 1760's. It lies in the township of Hague of which tiny settlement the good captain became a leading citizen. One winter day Cap'n Sam decided to sail a load of grist to Bolton via the frozen narrows. The ice was glare. The redoubtable captain loaded his cutter, rigged a sail, picked up a pitch fork for rudder and fortified himself with a wee bit of grain in liquid form to make the trip more comfortable. The cutter sailed off with dispatch but the rudder and the skipper were not quite adequate. Try as he would Cap'n Sam couldn't avoid Vicars Island. The cutter met it head on and stopped but the Captain continued on through the air to be grounded at last in a snowbank. Stoddard wrote, "Captain Sam was always dignified and on this occasion 'tis said his manner of resting on the snowbank was remarkably impressive . . . he came out and set his radiant face homeward . . . a Sam abounding in such language as would set a mule driver up in business."

Huletts Landing lies tucked behind Elias Harris's Elephant Mt. Stoddard had this to say about the place in 1873: "(It) is one of the oldest settlements on the lake and still the wildest". His guidebook described a white farmhouse which stood at the foot of Elephant. Hirman Vowers lived there and liked to host sportsmen. Guests were also welcome at two farms a little to the north owned by Philander Hulett. This gentleman operated a commissary of sorts for campers as well.

From the turn of the century onward island camping became more and more popular. Soon the state appointed a special ranger for the islands. His headquarters were erected on Glen Island by then vacated of course by "The Cold Water Club". The first ranger was Mr. Jay Taylor who along with his redoubtable boat, "The Banshee", became an integral part of the narrows scene for many years.

There are of course many other islands with stories which can be found in old guidebooks or have been handed down verbally. Many islands saw action of some sort during the colonial wars and much earlier but such actions cannot be pin-pointed since islands were unnamed and largely uncharted. Today their popularity for vacation camping increases yearly, however campsites are now of necessity assigned. One can't just light on a likely island and "jes' set for a spell" as in the days of the narrows hotels and earlier.

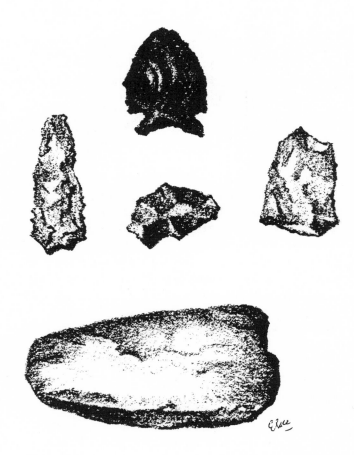

Found at Shelving Rock: spear and arrow points, flint chipping, stone celt or ax and lead musket ball flattened by impact.

90

Chapter 8

Sweet Peas and A White Bridge

Just beyond where once the north line of the Bradleys' property ran there's a lovely narrow thumb of a point. Long ago someone named this "Pearl Point". When the Hundred Island House opened in 1875 D.W. Sherman of Glens Falls was making plans to build the third hotel in the narrows there. He was a lumberman, merchandiser and hotelman, his father a pioneer lumber king who had made his fortune in the town on the Hudson River. The great mills of Glens Falls were doing an ever increasing business and that town was prospering.

The slopes of Shelving Rock behind Pearl Point like many others along the lake still showed their rocky ledges clearly for lumbermen had operated there not long before. However, as mentioned, the popularity of the lake as a resort area was turning the tide against further denuding of its shores and mountains even as the vast Adirondack forests along the upper Hudson were increasingly falling under ax and saw.

Pearl Point is formed by a little U-shaped bay to the south and a wide graceful sweep of land to the north above which rise the lake's highest mountains, Erebus and Black. Off the point the narrows are almost choked by islands of all shapes and

Northward from Pearl Point today

sizes, perhaps including the illusive quadrennial one!

Sherman's Pearl Point House opened in 1876, one year later than its close neighbor The Hundred Island House. Passengers on the Minne or Ganouskie saw its white shape rising like a frosted birthday cake from among tall trees with which the point was endowed. The frosting was actually a profusion of gingerbread woodwork which adorned any and all possible places from porches clear to the observatory roof. This form of ornamentation had become immensely popular and, to tell the truth had a certain charm of its own although what housepainters thought about it may have been less flattering.

As for the steamboats they now found two long piers reaching out below Shelving Rock about a half turn of the paddlewheels apart! Passengers also saw an arched white wooden bridge spanning the mouth of the U-shaped bay. It helped carry a footpath the few hundred feet to the Bradleys' hotel. The little bay itself was a perfect harbor for small craft and was lined with docks. Guests could stand on the bridge and watch the comings and goings below, even to what success a fisherman might have had! On some calm summer evenings the scene was unusually festive. A group of rowboats would set forth, each with a lighted Japanese lantern affixed to bow or stern. There would be the strumming of mandolins and guitars aboard. Reflected colors of those delicate lanterns streamed astern in the small ripples like a very wet water color or perhaps the scene could have been likened to a Japanese color print.

Canoes were certainly indigenous craft of earlier days on the lake but strangely enough they were hardly known at lake resorts until 1880. That year a group of enthusiasts set up camp on small islands near the head of the lake and organized the Eastern Canoe Association. The islands became known as "The Canoe Islands" while the very special magic of the little boats caught on quickly. Of course oldsters and local folk, especially followers of Izaak Walton, were not so easily persuaded. They continued to "hold with" the rowboat as might be expected.

It was apparent the lovely narrows could support three hotels in spite of the comparative isolation of the area. Steamboats played their part of course. It was about then, too, that nearby islands began to acquire cottages as described earlier. No doubt the presence and facilities of the hotels enhanced island living.

Sherman soon decided to enlarge his hotel for business was good. To be more accurate he elongated the place since the point was too narrow to build in any direction but toward the mainland. A large, pleasant dining room occupied much of the main floor addition. It had French doors along two sides opening onto the porches. Tables could be moved outdoors easily when the local mosquito and black fly population was either gone or not too hungry. Two cottage annexes were also added, one at the head of the little bay.

In the early 1890's my maternal grandfather brought his little family to Pearl Point. Their choice between the Shelving Rock hotels had, as I was always told, been determined by the flip of a coin. They journeyed up from New York City by Hudson River nightboat, train to Caldwell and lake steamboat. This took all of eighteen hours not counting the trip from a Brooklyn brownstone home to Manhattan over the fabulous new Brooklyn Bridge then scarce a decade old. The family continued to come to Pearl Point for some twelve or thirteen years during which mother and her sister grew from childhood to young womanhood. Just when

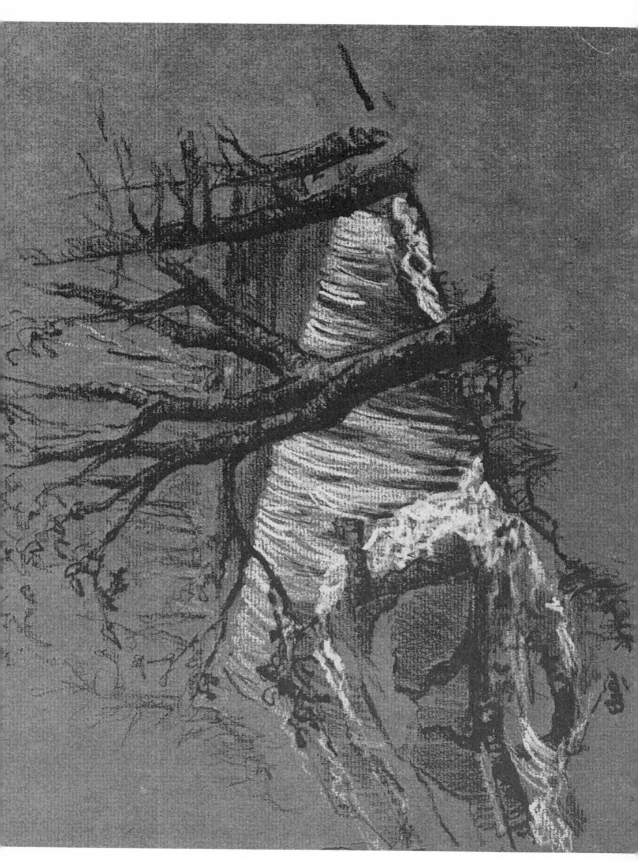

Dam at Shelving Rock Falls today

my father's family also came I do not know but it was in the later years that mother and father came to know well the famous "witching waves" the hotel's dining room floor developed!

The elongation had been built across a hollow between ledges. The hollow area itself became the unquestioned domain of gentlemen for it housed the billiard room. In those days pool, billiards and ladies simply didn't mix, at least not publicly. There gentlemen could smoke their cigars and pipes till the air was blueish while discussing matters as were of little concern, interest, or perhaps sometimes propriety for ladies to hear.

As time went by the timbering of this section, which supported the dining room floor above, began to settle a bit here and there. The result was that the floor acquired a sort of wavy surface. Dances were held in the dining room. By the time my parents-to-be came to trip the light fantastic toe there, they said it was something of an adventure. This didn't diminish the popularity of the dances though. The French doors would be thrown open to cool breezes off the lake, breezes laden with the pungent scents of down drafts off forested slopes. Often enough the air was also laden with the delicate scent of sweet peas. The flowers had arrived in this way. There was an enterprising woman who for many years made it her business to know when lake hotels held their weekly dances. She'd arrive that day on the morning steamer carrying baskets full of tiny corsages for gentlemen to present to the ladies of their choice that evening. The flowers might be violets or roses but most often they were sweet peas. There were of course no florists let alone shops of any kind in the area. She was called by some "the flower lady" but more often and realistically "Old Lady Brown". Indeed her considerable bulk was neither willowy nor otherwise flowerlike. That bulk settled comfortably on the hotel porch, she'd sell her fragrant wares until the returning steamer came along and carried her off again. Where she came from no one could ever tell me but I've heard Mother and others speak of her many times. I gather Mother often wore her flowers.

There were many pleasures for guests at Pearl Point. Aside from the sports it became a custom of a Sunday morning for those who did not attend any of the rather distant churches to row or paddle to Paradise Bay. Arrived in the quiet bay someone would lead in the singing of familiar hymns. For those who did wish to attend church a special "church boat" was operated, picking up passengers for Bolton at the various piers. "The Lake George Mirror", a weekly still very much alive, reported tennis tournaments, baseball and masquerades at the Shelving Rock resort. In the absence of nearby shops the latter events demanded quite a bit of hilarious ingenuity! As for tennis, it was popular with ladies too. How they managed to cover the court in ankle length skirts is a mystery but cover it they did and there were excellent players among them.

As for my family, in due time my grandfather bought a lovely rocky point a little to the south and built a summer home on it. With two grandchildren already on the scene and the probability of more he felt that a hotel would be difficult for the young mothers. Pearl Point remained the social center however, until its demise. The hotel also kindly acted as a commissary for meat and other perishables as well as being the postal address. It was the only one of the narrows hotels still extant in my lifetime, but my memory of it is that of a very young child. Sometimes I'd be allowed to stick my small nose over the hotel desk and ask for mail but I was far too young for social events. To tell the truth my clearest memory is of the kitchens and larders and it is an olfactory one rather than visual. Those regions smelled awfully good! Bread would be a-baking, roasts or soups gave off delicious aromas, there was a milky-buttery smell and all of it combined with that of hot water and soap with which the wide boarded floors were scrubbed to whiteness.

Of course I remember steamboat time. What child wouldn't! There was excitement, laughter, tension, joy, and sometimes tears at a departure.

In Pearl Point's later years rowboats and canoes were in the care of a dockman known as "Curly" due to the sun bleached thatch of hair which topped his long thin face. He was a tall splinter of a man whose eye corners were crinkled as are those of many who spend a lifetime outdoors. Curly became as much a part of the place as was Miss Jane of the Hundred Island House. He was also expected to meet the steamboats and attend to all baggage and freight. In this capacity he soon became a sort of unofficial reception committee of one. As the big sidewheelers came in Curly snubbed the huge hawsers thrown him while engaging in communications with the crews which added zest to life on both sides. They shared a mutual annoyance. There always seemed to be young daredevils among hotel guests who waited their chances to climb unnoticed over the rails and decks of the steamers clear to the hurricane deck. The objective was then to dive gloriously, or so they hoped, into the foaming wake when the steamer pulled away. The practice was dangerous, perhaps more so than they realized. The suction of the giant paddlewheels and maelstrom they created could easily prove too much for a swimmer let alone the dive itself. The steamboat company wasn't looking for trouble nor was the hotel. Consequently Curly and the crews had some lively chases aboard with a frowning captain watching from above.

Although there were no shops in or near the narrows hotels for the ladies to enjoy there were days each season when a hotel parlor would become unusually interesting. This was due to the arrival by morning steamer of a drummer toting worn and bulging suitcases. In a twinkling after his coming the parlor would be a wonderland of his wares and they were often beautiful and quite costly. Among tempting items were damasks, laces, fans, intricately embroidered linens from handkerchiefs to table cloths and other things of rich silks and satins from the world over. When the steamboat returned, all the finery that was unsold was packed and gone as expeditiously as Cinderella disappeared at the stroke of midnight.

There was another who peddled his wares at the hotels for many years but he rowed himself about in a little boat as weatherbeaten as his bronze face. This was an Indian who lived with his family in Bolton Landing. Continuing ancestral art the family gathered sweet grass each year which they wove into baskets of all shapes and sizes during the long winters. All old Adirondackers must remember such baskets since they were made and sold all through the mountains. The sweet smell of them is as unforgettable as the variety of their shapes and designs. After the rowboat and its wrinkled occupant had come by, many a basket appeared on hotel porches holding fancy work or mending or sat fragrantly on a dressing table full of buttons and bows.

To this day the sight or unmistakable smell of such a basket brings to me instantaneously the recollection of my grandmother in her favorite rocking chair on our porch. From out a sweet grass basket on a table nearby ran the finest of crochet thread which her busy hook was working into delicate lace that was to become an heirloom. That loop of thread from the table to her hands created a sort of no-man's-land on the porch which we children and the family dogs learned by experience to respect!

The Pearl Point House and most others along the lake couldn't boast of such sophistication and grandeur as possessed by a contemporary, the (second) Ft. William Henry Hotel at Caldwell. This great pile of turrets, balconies, enormous verandahs and gingerbread woodwork resembled and almost outdid the famous Saratoga Spa hotels. Hot and cold water was piped to all parts of it, there were telegraphed reports daily from the New York Stock Exchange and some guests kept private carriages, horses and grooms there for the season. The entire house was lighted by gas made on the premises as early as the 1870s! As to the building, considered so ultra ultra, Wm. Chapman White in his "Adirondack Country" remarked later; "Either it was designed by no architect, by a mad architect...or it just accumulated!" Its four to six stories certainly presented a staggering admixture of architectural styles.

The narrows hotels were more homelike, haute couture was not demanded of their guests, nor desired. No account of Pearl Point would be complete without mention of the single small bath tub the place had. This fixture lay around at Shelving Rock long after the hotel was razed, not yet an antique but an object of some kind of sentiment. Originally it was located upstairs directly over the boiler room which gave users the double treat of a steambath as well. Furthermore, guests had to make an appointment with the thing since, of course, it was in quite constant demand. Also they had to pay the sum of 25¢ for a bath in it doubtless due to the need for extra stoking below.

The narrows hotels were still young when an organization was born on the lake which was way ahead of its time as time has proved. In 1885 sixteen citizens got together to promote better observation of game laws. By 1889 other matters were taken up by the increasing membership of the organization. The primary one was pollution! Sanitary checks resulted along the entire lake and controls were established long before the matter became of the widespread concern which it is today. The controls applied also to the lake's watershed. The organization took the name of "Lake George Association" in 1909 and was also responsible among other things for the first navigation spindles placed along the lake. The motor boat had arrived on the scene.

Pearl Point, of all the other narrows hotels, survived into the 'gasoline age'. Wealthier people had long enjoyed private steam yachts. These required the employment of captain and engineer. The naphtha launch followed but it was the gasoline powered engine which ultimately placed motorized navigation within the reach of more people.

The early launches were graceful, V-bottomed boats, their hulls heavy and extremely well built in most cases. They shone with brass fittings and polished decks of golden oak, mahogany or even more exotic woods like rosewood. Flag poles almost scratched the sky and gay awning striped tops frequently with fringes like a surrey's could be put up with about the ease of a similar operation on early touring cars. Their gaiety however went well with picture hats, parasols, white flannels and boaters!

The boat lights burned kerosene and of course had to be lighted by hand. This was no small feat on a windy night, especially since there were no windshields. It was the engines themselves, though, which set those boats in a particular corner of old-

Oiling and priming cans for early motorboats.

timers' memories. To say the least they were temperamental as were the steam engines of a century earlier. They were demanding and frustrating, each an outright individualist with a disposition all its own. Engines were not decked over for there had to be access to them for operation. They sat gloriously in full view with a confounding mass of protuberences that were petcocks, throttle and spark levers, gears, grease cups and a large flywheel. Self starters were things of the future so that the motor had to be started manually by a quick spin of the flywheel. Before this operation began each small petcock above the cylinders had to be opened and primed with gas. It was also wise to check the grease cups which lived, as I recall, somewhere down near the bilge. They ate an unpleasant yellowish grease. Starting the motor really required perseverance, muscle and a fair amount of agility. The boatman squatted or bent double at the forward end of the engine where the flywheel was located. In spite of all the priming and greasing and setting the spark an immediate start by spinning that flywheel was more theory than fact most often. The motor might give a feeble cough and lapse into silence again and this could go on for a long time. Then the engine would be flooded requiring another maneuver. The little petcocks would have to be reopened, then 'blown out'. This produced a hissing noise which was one of those noises one never forgets. Child though I was at the time, if I heard it now I'd recognize it instantly.

When man finally triumphed over matter the skipper had to leap to the opposite end of the engine where spark, throttle, and gear were set as well as the steering wheel. It was a little complicated for the earliest boats had no reverse. It was always well to aim the bow with forethought or disaster might result. Then reversible propellers were devised but it was difficult if at all possible to get these characters into neutral, again a disconcerting thing to a nervous boatman confronted with spark and throttle levers as well. When self starters were invented things got a bit easier.

My mother, aunt and neighbors often worked hard over a flywheel of our first launch type Fay-Bowen when menfolk were back at business in the city. The boat was indispensible for marketing expeditions so that even the maids were sometimes called to action to spell the others. About everyone took a turn at the flywheel except my grandmother. She loved to look out over the water but would have as little to do with boats as possible. When she had crossed the ocean as a very young girl she had been shipwrecked off the coast of Britain and never afterwards trusted water for travelling purposes. All this aside, engines were completely out of her province anyway, and as far as she was concerned would remain so! When she did have to cross the lake on rare occasions someone would always hand her the bow rope to hold. For some inexplicable reason this seemed to give her a sense of control over her fate.

It should be added that in spite of all the drawbacks if you ask any oldtimer about his first motor boat you'll still detect a measure of fierce pride and deep affection even today.

As to the private steam yachts whose era overlapped that of the motor boat they were indeed luxurious, often over 80 ft. in length. One of them was very famous in her day. This was the "Ellide" built for E. Burgess Warren who had a summer home on Green Island. Slim as the proverbial matchstick, she was built for speed and attained it! Her top speed of a little over 40 MPH set not only a lake but a world record. Old lakers recalled one attempt at a record made over a course off Green Island. The course was held to exactly a mile and no more for fear her boilers might blow up.

One of the early motor boats was owned by a young minister who later became a bishop of the Episcopal church and prominent resident of the Bolton Landing area. Even then he was an ardent fisherman, eager to fish the narrows. On the boat's initial run a group of worthy gentlemen assembled on the Sagamore Hotel dock to watch her pass. She passed proudly around the pier and headed into the narrows. Some of the observers reserved judgement nevertheless. On reaching a desired spot at the entrance to the narrows the young minister decided to anchor. He put the boat briefly into reverse then discovered that somehow the gears had jammed and he couldn't get her out of reverse again. Due to this turn of events the young man decided for home. Gentlemen still watching on the pier looked at each other mystified.

"It would almost seem, Sir, unless my eyes deceive me, that the boat is returning stern first!"

"Indeed yes, her image is getting larger. What an extraordinary way to navigate!"

They watched dumbfounded as return the boat did stern first. Rounding the dock at last, in this manner, she backed carefully into her slip while the gentlemen began to expound on the relative efficacy of steam! The Sagamore Hotel behind them was, incidentally the second of that name to occupy Green Island. It burned in 1914 to be replaced a little later by the present building.

Comments and notices in "The Lake George Mirror" reflected the changes motorization was bringing to the lake. That weekly liked to advertise itself as (in the 1890s) "one of the handsomest journals of watering places published . . . its pages devoted to light reading of the most approved watering place gossip. No Scandal"!

In the early 20th century the Mirror noted with possible alarm a new trend it labelled "automobilitis". It added that "the disease seems to be spreading!" In the issue of August 7, 1908 it printed this warning to auto enthusiasts: "Notice is hereby given that through the co-operation of the towns of Caldwell and Bolton and citizens along the (Bolton) road the road is, during the season, policed...maximum speeds through villages and where thickly settled 10 MPH, on bridges, grades and sharp curves 4 MPH, under any circumstances 20 MPH, slower speeds required in dust, when passing vehicles, etc." There was moreover a law which stated that when an auto met a horse drawn vehicle the driver of the former must stop and shut off his motor if the driver of the latter held up his hand to indicate a nervous horse.

The Bolton Supply Store still advertised "wagons of quality $36.50". Englanders haberdashery of Glens Falls were abreast of the times. They offered "clothes for the motorist, dusters $1.50 to $8, gauntlet gloves $1 to $4, auto shirts of rubber $5, caps in great variety 50¢ to $2.50". They felt the horseless carriage had come to stay, as it did.

Ziebach's Drug Store at Caldwell sold: "Pure drugs and Sundries, patent medicines, oils and paints, alcoholic beverages and the famous Ziebach soda".

Again in Glens Falls, Fowler's Department Store had "the pride of all corsetries...with invisible front lacings...absolutely essential in supplying that svelte slenderness, that non-hip slimness, that sinuous absence of adiposity (?) so necessary to princess and sheath gowns". And that, apparently was what the ladies of fashion were wearing!

Guests at Pearl Point could reach such emporiums only if they made a day of it. They would have to travel by early steamboat, then train or trolley. Few did. They arrived with well stocked trunks. There were other things to do nearby for which they had come to the lake. For example one couple who had come to the lake every year since their honeymoon here had a hobby which kept them busy. It resulted in a really fine chart. He would row and fish while she, shaded by a parasol sat in the stern taking soundings with a plumb line. The fish he kept bringing in gave many a hotel friend a fine meal while the map they eventually compiled showed not only depths but the nature of the bottom as well. This last is a very interesting subject among fishermen. My Grandfather prized his copy highly.

Another elderly gentleman among Grandfather's friends went off to paint at every opportunity. The canvases he produced were drawn well enough but unfortunately the artist was partially color blind. This resulted in some rather unusual scenes of the lake. When Grandfather built his summer cottage the old gentleman presented to him a scene done from the rocky point on which the house stood. Grandfather gallantly bought a nice mission oak display easel for it and we lived with it for quite a number of years.

As to the Pearl Point House it did survive all the other hotels in the narrows by some years. It finally closed its white, hospitable doors at the end of the 1918 season. In the previous summer the large Knapp home on the mountain above had burned, the towering flames sending showers of sparks and embers down onto the partially flat roof of Pearl Point. The old wooden hotel was perhaps saved by guests and employees who formed a bucket brigade from lake to roof dousing the sparks as they fell. The event might have nevertheless given the later owners of the hotel, the Rugge family of Glens Falls, food for thought. The building was no longer young nor up-to-date. Probably, most of all, times were changing, Pearl Point was not nor seemed likely ever to be on an automobile route.

The property was added to the Knapp Estate. All buildings, including two annex cottages, were removed excepting the original house on the point which Sherman built in 1876. This became for some years the summer home of George Knapp's son and his family. At last and with regret this building too was razed. It was no longer feasible to keep it in repair.

The arched white bridge across the little bay has long been gone too. On it quite a number of years ago a young man asked the lovely little lady of his choice to become his wife. She answered "yes". Perhaps that's why when I happen sometimes to be on Pearl Point on a gentle evening I could swear there come to me from somewhere the faint strains of a waltz and a delicate, illusive fragrance, the fragrance of a tiny corsage of sweet peas.

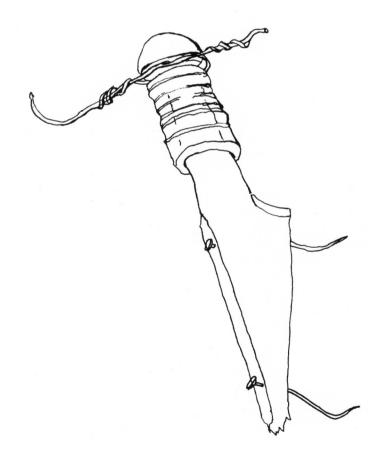

The telephone arrives.

Sunrise over Erebus Mountain from Gourd Island in the narrows.   *Photo by Richard Dean*

East Indian bungalow which stood on Hen and Chicken Island.

Naptha launch among the narrows' islands. Photo Courtesy of Mr. and Mrs. Ralph Lapham.

Ganouskie moored as saloon at Big Burnt Island. Lapham party passing in rowboat foreground. — Photo Courtesy of Mr. and Mrs. Ralph Lapham.

Hon. Jerome Lapham's home on Phantom Island. — Photo Courtesy of Mr. and Mrs. Ralph Lapham

Pearl Point Hotel and annex and the white bridge. Note lumbered slopes beyond.   *Stoddard Photo*

Pearl Point House.

The U-shaped harbor at Pearl Point. *Stoddard Photo*

Pearl Point from the north. *Stoddard Photo*

Steamer Horicon I landing at Pearl Point.   *Stoddard Photo*

Steamer and private steamboats and launches at Bolton.   *Photo by Thatcher*

Awaiting the steamer at Pearl Point. Author's mother second from left, mother's sister and sister-in-law on right.
Family Photo

The white bridge.   *Stoddard Photo*

1914 Gold Cup Regatta off Bolton. Mankowskie's "Ankle deep" extreme left.

E. Burgess Warren's world record holding "Ellide"

108

1903 launching of Steamer Sagamore at Pine Point, Caldwell [Lake George Village].   *Photo Courtesy of Philip Sullivan*

The Sagamore in the narrows.   *Family Photo*

George Reis and Anderson Bowers in Gold Cup Regatta winner "El Lagarto."

Famous motorboat "Whipoorwill" at Gold Cup Regatta in the 1930s.

Chapter 9

Paradise Was Almost Lost

North of Pearl Point the eastern shore of the narrows sweeps in a graceful arc below the lake's second highest mountain. The slopes are densely wooded and there are several beautiful rocky points on one of which the stone was quarried for the Knapp home on Shelving Rock. The mountain's shoulders drop so close to the water's edge that there's barely room for the old lumber road along shore. The mountain's name is "Erebus", a name somewhat incongruously out of Greek mythology. "Erebus", in ancient Greek legend, was supposedly a region deep within the earth through which the dead were thought to pass. Whoever named the mountain was obviously versed in mythology but whether the name was given due to frustration when ascending the deeply forested slopes or out of a wry sense of humor no one recorded for posterity. It's true enough that no one climbing Erebus will find panoramic views even from the summit. The dense timber might easily be thought to provide a sort of stygian shade all the way.

At the mountain's feet lies Paradise Bay whose beauty has made it the most famous excursion goal along the entire lake. Again, who compared it to Paradise I do not know, but unique it most certainly is. There was a brief time in the late

1870's when the bay's wild, unspoiled loveliness might have been altered but fortunately this did not happen. Most likely, too, at some point prior to that date lumbermen had been busy in the area and used Paradise Bay as a storage for timbers as they had Log Bay to the south. Perhaps even the bay's shores had been cut over but since then nothing has prevented the maturing of great native white pine, hemlock and some hardwood. It is the prevalent evergreens which help not only to shelter the almost land-locked bay but give its water a deep blue-green color making its depths somehow mysterious. The water of the bay is almost always calm for wind from any direction finds it hard to penetrate its ramparts. These consist of one end of a large peninsula, which also forms Red Rock Bay to the south, and two islands northward of the peninsula's tip. The narrow isthmus which connects the peninsula to the mainland tapers the waters of both bays so it doesn't require a ball players's arm to toss a stone from one bay into the other. It was this conformation of land which nearly changed the aspects of Paradise Bay back in the 1870's. While the two islands were always state land the mainland, including of course the peninsula, was not, until quite recently.

From about the mid to latter 19th century or early twentieth, huge tracts of the lake's eastern shores from Ticonderoga southward to Red Rock Bay were owned by The Horicon Iron Works. Business boomed for this Ticonderoga company during the Civil War as iron production boomed everywhere for the manufacture of munitions. The iron ore was mined along Lake Champlain where its presence had been determined as early as the 1740's by black sands along the lakeshore. As mentioned earlier charcoal was essential in the north country for refining the ore hence great tracts of timberland were a necessary adjunct. Probably much of the hardwood along Lake George fed the maws of five huge charcoal kilns along the lake's outlet. Each could swallow 65 cords at a time. President of the Horicon Iron Works was a versatile gentleman named Cyrus Butler.

When the war ended quantity iron production dropped sharply. In time the Horicon Iron Works virtually ceased operations and Mr. Butler, aware of the resorts being built in the narrows, thought long and hard about some of his company's land in that area. It was potentially a fine resort region. When the famous old Minne-Ha-Ha was finally retired from lake service in 1877 Butler bought her, minus engine and boilers. He had no need for these which in fact were shipped out to Vancouver B.C. and doubtless saw more service there.

Some few accounts say that Butler intended to live aboard the old steamboat himself but most agree that from the first he intended to make her into a unique floating hotel. This she indeed became but not in the originally chosen spot which was Paradise Bay. Butler thought it would be possible to cut through the isthmus and moor the boat in the subsequent channel. On the deeply indented peninsula he would build a summer cottage colony whose focal point for dining and social life would be the old Minne. However, the Minne was never towed to Paradise Bay. The project proved too difficult and costly. Butler shifted his plans and the Minne to another location quite nearby, as will be told later. Paradise Bay remained as nature intended and nothing was allowed to mar its beauty when some years later its mainland and the peninsula became part of the Knapp Estate. A loop of the lumbermen's road which passed the bay was levelled with stone retaining walls for Mr. Knapp's carriages but it was so unobtrusively done that the walls are hardly

Paradise Bay

visible from the water. The forest grew and grew in its natural cycles as it does today.

As years passed, rowboats and canoes of early vacationers began to meet more and more little steamers, naphtha launches and finally motor boats circling the bay's quiet waters for sight of its loveliness. Even small excursion steamers found they could enter and turn safely. The bay's entrances are three in number although two are the most often used. The two islands which help form the northerly channel are state picnic islands today but picnicking is prohibited on the mainland shores to preserve the wild beauty.

Not many years ago a well known summer resident of Bolton undertook to carry guests from a nearby hotel on boat tours of the lake. Paradise Bay was of course a high point of the excursions. Sometimes the erstwhile guide felt that his passengers were not sufficiently impressed with the beauty of his beloved lake. On such trips, once inside the magnificent bay, he was apt to stop his boat's motor, lean over the gunwale and gaze quietly and soberly into the depths of that blue-green water. The dim outlines of old sunken logs could be indistinctly seen down there. When his passengers were fully alerted and wondering what might be below he would point out the logs. He would then ask portentiously;

"Know what those are? Those are caskets! It's an old, old lake custom that if one lived a worthy life, lived worthily mind you, one could be buried here in Paradise if one wished to be!"

Having delivered this solemn information he would start the motor again and depart the hallowed waters slowly and in reverent silence. Quite possibly some people believed him for George Reis, while an expert racing boat driver, was also a good actor, for years closely associated with the famed Pasadena (Cal) Playhouse. As to his racing fame he was three times winner of the great Gold Cup Regatta. Thus the famous race was run off Bolton Landing for three years in the 1930's since it was always held on the winner's home waters. It was not, as a matter of fact, the first time the race was run on this lake. In 1914 Count Casimir Mankowski, summer resident of Bolton, defended his title over the same course. His boat, the Ankle Deep, unfortunately struck a floating timber and was out of the race.

George Reis's famous boat El Lagarto or "Leaping Lizard" literally leapt to victory over Lake George's waves twice, piloted by her owner and Commander Anderson "Dick" Bowers. The third year misfortune put her out of the race. The famous "Lizard" can be seen today at the Adirondack Museum, Blue Mt. Lake. However, like the steamboats' whistles and the beautiful rhythm of the Bellingers' oars, the unmistakable growling roar of El Lagarto's single engine will never be forgotten by anyone who heard it or had the thrill of riding in her on this lake.

Most visitors see Paradise Bay in full daylight. Yet such places are at their finest in the illusory hours or moments, for example at daybreak when the eastern mountains are first outlined with glowing light, or at dusk when the ventriloquistic Hermit Thrush pours out his song as images blur. Then there's the special phantom light when the moon rises like a huge lamp over the black slopes and its light begins to trickle through the treetops to set the water sparkling and the scent of evergreens is strong and cool. There are times after a rain when mists rise off the water wavering like manes of galloping horses and on Erebus above one can see clouds being born. The shores have no sharp delineations then, they blend into the quiet water and mystery and imagination can walk hand in hand.

114

"Weathered stump from the shallows."

115

The narrow isthmus is a fine drinking place for deer. Here too forget-me-nots find the muddy bottom to their liking, their lovely blue seeming like tiny specks of sky fallen to earth. Long legged herons inspect the shallows with dignified precise strides and I've seen the great grandfather of all turtles taking a sun bath on a ledge.

In the bay's windless coves the magnificent white water lilies of the northland grow in safety. Their round rubbery leaves are often resting places for gauzey winged dragon flies and sometimes frogs. The more fearless frogs sit eyeing man with oriental inscrutability as if they have grave reservations about these two-legged creatures...which perhaps they do!

An Adirondack Indian legend tells of the origin of the lilies. It claims they hold the soul and heart of an Indian maid who once loved a young chieftain named "Sun". Her love was hopeless for he was promised to another by tribal law. One evening the heartbroken girl got into her canoe and paddled away down a wilderness lake never to be seen again. On the lake the next morning her saddened people were astounded to see the water's surface covered with fragrant lilies no one had seen there before. Strangely enough the flowers closed each day at dusk when the heavenly sun was gone to open again each dawn when it rose.

Winter dresses Paradise Bay in austere beauty. It would almost seem that time had stopped in that quiet place but for a sense of something held deep down that is never rigid as ice nor even cold.

"Cedar decoration of an old gazebo"

Chapter 10

French Point

The western shores of the narrows are formed by the precipitous Tongue Mt. Range. These mountains split the wide southerly basin of the lake in two, north of Bolton. To the east lie the narrows of the main lake, to the west is a deep bay known as Northwest (once Ganouskie) Bay. This bay was often mistaken in colonial days as the water route northward only showing itself a cul-de-sac after several miles travel. In pre-glacial times it was down this valley that the southbound stream flowed out of the mountain barrier.

While lumbermen were once active on the westerly slopes of the Tongue Range there was never a road along its shores. Today there is a hiking trail over the mountain crests only one of whose feeder trails ascends from the narrows. This is reachable to all intents and purposes only by boat. In spite of the ruggedness of the area there was a hotel on the narrows side along this shore.

The tapering tongue of the range gives it its name, the tip of that tongue long being known as Montcalm Point. It was on emerging from the narrows here that the French general, Montcalm, first saw pre-arranged signal fires above the present Bolton. They'd been lighted to assure him that a portion of his troops sent overland from Ticonderoga had managed the difficult journey over the mountain range. Most of the army was waterborne, their goal an attack on the British at Ft. William Henry. Montcalm had a combined force of over 7,600 men including over 1,000 Indian allies. The poor devils sent over land had hacked and hauled their way over the untracked, densely wooded and insect infested mountains, a back breaking task. The route they hewed roughly was that of the present skillfully engineered Tongue Mt. Highway. A colorful picture of Montcalm's expedition was drawn by 19th century historian Francis Parkman as follows:

"As evening drew near was seen one of those wild pageantries of war Lake George often witnessed. A restless multitude of birch bark canoes filled with painted warriors glided by the shores and islands like troops of water fowl. Two hundred and fifty bateaux came next moved by sail and oar, some bearing Canadian militia and some the battalions of Old France in trim and gay attire . . . then the cannon and mortars, the provision bateaux and field hospital. Under the flush of sunset they held their course along the romantic lake to play their part in the historic drama which lends a stern enchantment to its fascinating scenery. They passed the narrows in the mist and darkness and when a little before dawn they rounded the promontory of Tongue Mt. they saw on the right three fiery sparks shining!" Of course the latter were the signal fires. The army now proceeded in the attack on the British fort. The massacre after its surrender cast a great blot on Montcalm's reputation although it is said he did his utmost to halt it. Cooper tells of this whole affair in "The Last Of The Mohicans".

Most of the western narrows' shore must look today much as this army saw it over two hundred years ago. A single thread of summer cottages now stretches north from Montcalm Point for a mile or two backed against the steep slopes of the mountains, beautiful but uncompromising mountains. Beyond the last cottage the terrain is wild and steeper with one fairly level point of some 40 acres protruding into the waters of the narrows. This is French Point. Whether or not French soldiers or scouts ever actually camped there is one of those questions lost to local history. It's most likely they did since the rest of that shoreline affords no tenable resting place for a body of men in the event of foul weather or for tactical reasons. It was on French Point that a hotel was built shortly after the Shelving Rock hotels had been established and about the time Cyrus Butler was looking over the possibilities at Paradise Bay just across the water.

The hotel was named The Sherman House after its first owner Mrs. William Sherman. Aside from several annex cottages near the hotel the point was large enough to support a small farm which provided fine fresh foodstuffs. The age of great commercial refrigeration was in the future! If the Point might seem to have been even more isolated than the hotels at Shelving Rock with no road whatsoever reaching the place it must be remembered that almost all lake resorts were reached and served by the steamboats, not roads. The latter, if they existed at all, were dusty, bumpy and slow, all in all not a very comfortable way of travel. The steamers could land at French Point as easily as anywhere else. The Sherman House not only had a beautiful location mid-way of the narrows but was also reputedly near what Stoddard called "those mythical places known as the best fishing grounds"!

Mrs. Sherman was faced with one problem which was present but far less acute at the other hotels. Long before Father Joques saw the lake, probably long before the first Indian canoes used its waters, the ancestors of Old Dick's "rattel snaikes" found the ledges and talus of the Tongue Range ideal for homesteading! Their descendants have remained of the same opinion down through the years and they don't always stay in their own front yards. This is particularly true in hot, dry weather. When the leaves of aspens are the size of a mouse's ear in spring these characters emerge from their dens, or so it's said. Mrs. Sherman engaged a special snake hunter such as Old Dick had been, a man well versed in the habits of snakes. He unobtrusively patrolled the grounds apparently with success for snakes were never a determent to the hotel's popularity.

Once years later my mother and a friend stopped to pass the time of day with an old gentleman who then resided in a weatherbeaten house in the hills near Bolton. He had quite a reputation as a snake hunter so naturally the talk drifted that way. He explained to them how he could often track snakes as other hunters track their quarries. Snakes leave unmistakable wiggly marks as well as depressions where they've coiled. He knew where many a den was located such as those on the Tongue Range. He'd devised an implement to snare them consisting of a broom length pole with pincers at the end which could be snapped shut from the handle much as a tree pruner operates. The old man said that as a very youn'un he'd been employed at that old hotel at French Point to keep the place free of snakes.

The old hunter loved newspapers. After he'd looked at them he papered the walls of his home with them for insulation, layer on layer. A day by day history of the world kept the drafts out of his house! His name was Will Clark. Some years prior to my mother's visit he'd taken author Carl Carmer on a local snake hunt. Carmer later devoted a chapter to this experience in his book on New York State entitled "Listen For A Lonesome Drum."

The interlaced paths around French Point were dotted with the inevitable little gazebos. I don't mean to disparage the latter for they had great charm, being delightful places to sit and visit, read, crochet or embroider or just contemplate. Few survive along the lake today, one of which, in the narrows area, many people have still enjoyed recently. It is the one which sits perched atop a sheer rock above Shelving Rock Falls. At the date of this writing its fanciful construction is known to many vacationers to whom the present Knapp property on which it stands has never been closed. Probably built after the Hundred Island House was bought by George Knapp, its benches and rails are witness to a time worn custom. They are inscribed with hundreds of initials carved by visitors through the years, some carefully cut, others crude. The story connected with the little building is not however concerned with these. It deals with the actual construction of the little gazebo. The eaves, cornices and balustrades of the tiny structure are adorned with natural, fantastically gnarled roots and branches suggesting that the builder had a high degree of imagination! In the shapes can be seen all sorts of creatures, real and unreal. It's said that the man who built it made one stipulation. Every other day he required a gallon of alcohol which he said "would preserve the wood"! On seeing the completed structure a local theory rose that not only the wood had received the preservative. Whatever the most efficacious use of the alcohol may have been it's God's truth that the wee house with all its strange creatures has withstood ice, snow, rain, heat and the ceaseless spray and mist of the waterfall these many years with remarkable

Gazebo at Shelving Rock Falls

stability and aplomb!*

The Sherman House was destroyed by fire, the arch enemy of isolated locations, in 1889. The Point, with one of the survivng cottages, became a private summer home for a number of years. Thereafter it was purchased by the General Electric Company of Schenectady as a summer vacation camp for women employees. Today like the Tongue Mt. Range behind it French Point belongs to the state. It was given to the people in memory of George Foster Peabody.

Early in the present century the wild steep shores north of French point were home to a man about whom many a tale is still told. Cap'n Sam Patchen and his cutter attained fame in the writings of S.R. Stoddard. I'm sure Mr. Stoddard would have added Henry Durrin to his list had he known him. Henry lived for some years in a tiny cabin whose site lay near the Dollar Islands, scene of that episode in "The Last Of The Mohicans". There the ledges of the mountain range reach climactic beauty, the rock dropping sheerly downward and out of sight in the water. Only one with the agility of a mountain goat would be at home along this stretch.

Most people called Henry Durrin "Hank". His chosen way of life was close to Indian ways and some always believed he was part Indian although others say this was not so. Whatever the truth Hank married an Indian woman and the two lived for most of their married life in the house beside Shelving Rock Falls. How long the marriage lasted I'm not quite sure. Hank hunted and fished the narrows area as he chose.

One day he shot a bear on Black Mountain. The bear had two cubs which Hank decided to take home with him. He got hold of both but on the way home they most tore his shirt and hide to shreds. He kept them nevertheless, chaining them to a pole outdoors or in the old barn below the house which still stands (1973). When Hank was away he got his neighbors' youngsters to come down the mountain road and feed his "pets". Young Laura Benton (Mrs. Jesse Stiles of Ft. Ann) and her brother performed this kindness but one day found one of the bears had gotten loose in the barn. They had quite a time and employed various stratagems to get the animal chained again. The Benton Farm was located about halfway between Hogtown and Shelving Rock Falls so the young people had quite a walk to begin with.

There's another who remembers Hank and his bears vividly. When the Bentons moved elsewhere George Marvanville and his wife moved onto their farm. They brought with them a tiny boy who was "own cousin" to them both. The child's mother had died at his birth. The father was a lumberman whose other children were still too young to care for an infant. Hank remained a neighbor down the mountain road at the falls. When he called on his neighbors he had a habit of bringing one of the bears along. He'd taught the bear to perform a "dance", rising on his hind legs and waving those formidable paws in the air! The little toddler, far from being amused was scared half to death and always immensely glad when his foster mother gave the bear a precious loaf of bread and man and animal would

---

*In June of 1974 the little gazebo which sat overlooking Shelving Rock Falls for some 80 odd years went on a trip. To be exact it went on a hay ride. Its new site is near the present Knapp home where it will be affectionately preserved. The seemingly impossible feat of moving it all in one piece was accomplished by Mr. George Stiles, formerly of Shelving Rock and Mr. Ralph Stiles, present caretaker of the Knapp property. Moving it up the steep trail to the wood road showed the ingenuity, determination and long-time knowhow of the two gentlemen for not a single tree of size was felled. The men were aided by one not-so-young jeep, sundry oiled timbers and a local hay wagon on which the little building completed its journey. When all was done George Stiles remarked very calmly. "If I hadn't known we could do it I never would have started it"! As for the gazebo, not one of its fantastic creatures was lost since the little building proved as sturdy as the day it was built.

121

depart again. Many years later the little boy became John Stiles' successor as caretaker of the Knapp Estate on which he had lived and worked many years under John. Even as a little lad he had known the enormous ripping power of a bear's claws! His name is Ernest Granger.

When Ernest wasn't very old his foster father became caretaker of the General Electric camp at French Point. The boy's initiation as a boatman began then. One of the lad's seasonal chores was herding several cows aboard a scow. The animals were transported down through the narrows to French Point where they supplied milk for the camp all summer. Ernest's four-legged passengers weren't keen about the trip he recollects and probably expressed themselves vocally on the way as the scow was towed through the island channels.

Incidentally such scows were time worn work horses all along the lake for years. Steamboats, and later on motor boats, towed them laden with all sorts of cumbersome loads, building stone, coal, lumber, live stock, barrels of this and that, bricks and many other things. Towing them could be tricky business on a lake where winds rise suddenly and bounce off land unpredictably. The scows could become very wayward characters!

Ernest Granger married Susie, one of Jack Dacy's four daughters. They'd known each other since both attended the little school in Hogtown as young children. As for Ernest's memory of Hank Durrin, he continued to encounter him on the lake long after Hank no longer lived at Shelving Rock Falls.

If Hank's bears frightened a small boy it was not to the extent that another member of the family ursidae reputedly scared two grown hunters who according to local story first came upon the famous bears' den on the lakeward shoulders of Sleeping Beauty Mountain. On finding the low opening in a small cliff face they decided to go home, fetch lanterns and explore its depth. They took their guns with them too. The low tunnel opened into a sizable chamber. Before they got to looking around a scraping and growling warned them of another presence! Greatly alarmed one of the men discharged his gun in the direction of the noises. The percussion doused the lanterns leaving the cave totally dark. The hunters had but one common thought, to get out fast. Groping their way once again on all fours one of them suddenly yelled;

"Hey! Quit yer shovin', I'm going out fast as I kin!"

An answer came from outside;

"God A'mightly, I ain't shovin ye, I be outside a'ready. It's the old she-bar is after ye. Git out here, I got my gun ready!"

His friend emerged with alacrity followed by the she-bar with her jaws open! She was dispatched without being able to contend that one's home, be it man's or animal's is supposed to be one's castle.

I have been in the bears' den several times so can vouch for its existence without question. As to the story of its discovery the above is the best known version. A trail eventually ran to th den but, since the forest has it subtle way of changing, the den is no longer easy to find.

To return to Hank Durrin, he and his wife eventually parted. This gave rise to another local tale which was based on Hank's well known sometimes irascible nature. Supposedly very angered by his wife for some reason or other, which he often was, the story says he tied her to a lone tree on little Arrow Island south of Red

The Old Barn — Shelving Rock Falls

Rock Bay. The tale insists that it was a very cold day in early winter when every wave that washed over the island coated everything on it with ice, including Mrs. Durrin. Claiming that she was part Eskimo and thus inured to this sort of intense cold it's said she suffered no harm after managing to free herself. However she thereupon decided to leave her spouse. Actually Mrs. Durrin was three times her husband's size and by no means a helpless character in her own right. It would certainly have been quite a feat for Hank to have pulled off, but the story was a favorite around Shelving Rock.

When the couple separated Hank betook himself to a tiny cabin on that steep shore north of French Point. From there he hunted and fished the narrows as before. One day he hit on an idea. In order to flush game from its hiding place he got hold of an old auto klaxon. He strapped its battery across his shoulders and set forth blowing the thing for all it was worth. Without doubt birds and beasts responded as desired but other hunters who happened to be in the area began to doubt their sanity.

Hank had assumed squatters rights to his cabin site which was on state land. When the cottages on the islands received their conge Hank's domicile was not exempt. With a shrug, knowing that he couldn't argue with the state, Hank moved again. His cabin was burned. The old lumbermen's house near Black Mt. Point was still standing although long abandoned. Hank moved in. It was from there that he would skate up-lake past Ernest and Susie Granger's home in Lovers' Lane although he cut overland at this point knowing the thin ice likely in that channel. He'd be wearing enormously long wide-bladed skates and be pushing a sled with high curling runners. In this were meat and pelts he would trade for such few things he needed from civilization. He'd not forgotten old Shelving Rock neighbors for sometimes he agreed to deliver a load of Jack Dacy's fine potatoes over the ice in this manner.

By spring anyone who chanced to pass Hank's adopted home was met by an extraordinary sight. Every shrub and low hanging branch nearby was festooned with a spiney porcupine hide. Most probably Hank didn't mind the meat, in fact may have found it quite palatable the while it could easily be acquired without the waste of valuable ammunition! Perhaps Hank simply didn't like porcupines and when he didn't like something or someone he was not apt to change his opinion. In the case of fellow humans he just acted as though they weren't there. Whatever the case a staple of Hank's diet was obvious.

The Durrins had a son. He achieved a measure of fame as an athlete with paddle and canoe. "Sherm" Durrin won a place on the United States Olympic Canoe Team earlier in this century. His expertise was proved locally one summer when a canoe race was run off Bolton Landing. It had attracted many a young college athlete, summer visitor and good canoeist. A well known Boltonite mentioned earlier gleefully went in search of Sherm and persuaded him to enter the race. Young Durrin strolled to the starting place in his work-a-day clothes, stepped most casually into his canoe and proceeded to hopelessly outdistance all other competitors before the race was half over.

Sherm didn't have a long life. He died at the age of 34. He went to a dance in Warrensburg one terribly cold winter night and on the way home felt drowsy. He pulled his car off the road for a nap. His frozen body was found in the car next morning.

As for the father, it's locally believed that Henry Durrin spent his declining years in or near Lake George Village, died there and is buried there. Aside from his hunting and fishing, Hank was an expert woodworker. This is attested to by the fact that he often helped Fred Smith Sr. of Bolton Landing in the making of those fine rowboats which are collectors items today. James Smith, one of Fred's sons, adds that Hank was of invaluable help to his father when Hank "decided to put his mind to it"!

Since eagles, birds of true wilderness places, are now seldom seen to soar over Amphitheater Bay and the little cabin site nearby, perhaps too, such men as the Durrins would find encroaching effects of motorization difficult to accept. Free spirits all, they may be happier somewhere else.

The beauty of a root.

Chapter 11

A Hotel and Its Mountain

The last hotel to be built in the wild, lovely narrows of the lake stood at the foot of Black Mountain. It was not only the last but perhaps fewer people today have knowledge of its existence than of any of the others. This isn't because of any lack of popularity, for it was a most charming place, but because its lifetime was short and the forest moved in quickly. As with the Sherman House and the Knapp home on Shelving Rock, fire, the arch enemy of isolated establishments, destroyed it completely. Its lifespan was the decade of the 1880s.

Very few who climb Black Mt. today notice the forest swallowed foundation walls, twisted metal and scorched brick near the start of the trail above Black Mt. Point. The fine expanse of rolling lawn which swept down to the shore south of the point no longer exists even as a meadow. Only the old lumber road which served the lumber camp nearby is still there, coming up along shore from Shelving Rock some four miles south. The road always ended here but once doubled back in a loop before the hotel porch, a branch serving the stable to the rear. The lumber camp was the same in which Hank Durrin later took up residence.

If few are aware of the hotel site probably many who land at Black Mt. Point, now state land, see the sunken hull of a sizable boat in the north bay. The old beams are spreading apart but the grace of her is still evident and her name is familiar. These are the remains of the beloved Minne, the famous Minne-Ha-Ha I. Here she finally came to rest sometime in the early 1890s but not before she felt feet on her decks again and heard conversation and laughter.

Since Black Mt. is the highest along the lake, and for some distance around, it had begun to be a goal for climbers by the mid 19th century. These didn't have as easy a time of it though as today's hikers do. Somehow they had to reach the area by small boat. Guidebooks of the time suggested that lake steamboats would help by towing smaller craft for an added fee of 50 cents. Early adventurers could cast off and row ashore to what was then known as "Popple Point" where a lumber road started them upward. This was of course one of the many skidways and tote roads which laced the slopes, for lumbermen were busy in the entire area, but it led most directly upward toward the summit. It took climbers to Black Mt. Ponds, tiny specks of water which lie over the south shoulder of the big mountain. From there however the road betook itself off eastward through dense timber more interesting and profitable than the steep, partially bare ledges of the top third of the mountain. From the ponds there was no trail upward. Those headed for the summit had to scramble and pick their way as best they could.

At the time Black Mt. in its entirety was also part of the timberlands owned by the Horicon Iron Works of Ticonderoga as was the area at Paradise Bay. The hardwoods off the mountain helped feed the mighty hunger of the charcoal kilns at the lake's outlet. Lumbermen in those days were not bound by clean-up laws and careful controls. In consequence tops and branches and other brush were left where they had been lopped off and often became tinder dry. Great forest fires resulted started by lightning or human carelessness and Black Mt. became indeed black. In time, of course, the growth cycle of the forest began anew, as birch, poplar and blueberry bushes greened the slopes, eventually giving shelter to other trees. Seedling pines were the last to come back, as they usually are.

By the late 1870s production of iron had dwindled and almost ceased at the Horicon Works. The enterprising company president, Cyrus Butler, had found his plans for a resort in the Paradise Bay area not working out, as noted earlier. He was not discouraged but looked instead a little to the north at the tall mountain at whose feet lay another beautiful if much smaller point. Butler was aware that people liked to climb the mountain, that it would in fact be quite a drawing card. In short order he had his recent purchase, the Minne-Ha-Ha, towed not to Paradise Bay as originally planned, but to the bay behind what was now renamed "Black Mt. Point". There she was securely moored and her superstructure altered to provide rooms for some forty guests. Her dining facilities could handle many more since mountain climbers often came and went the same day after returning to a hearty meal aboard.

In 1879 Stoddard, in his guidebook of that year, listed the Minne among other lake hotels, no doubt the year she began her new career. His notice read, "Laughing Waters (Minne-Ha-Ha), Black Mt. Point. The Point is under the management of Capt. G.W. Tubbs, board per day $3, per week $10 to $14". This was comparable to other hotels along the lake. The notice added, "Fish dinners $1!" It was still possible then for Adirondack resorts to pride themselves on serving local game and

128

fish, a custom soon to be stopped by stringent laws which prohibited the commercial sale of same.

Of course while the Minne was being rebuilt Butler gave thought to a principle asset, the mountain. A good trail to the summit was essential. This was built, using the old lumber road as far as it ran upward. The zigzags up the last third of the climb were constructed to be safe for equestrians as well as hikers. It is the trail in use today but in hotel days a toll was charged for its use, probably to defray cost of building and maintenance. Hikers paid $1, riders $3.

Butler's plans were far from completed. A site had been chosen for a hotel at the foot of the trail and above the bay where the Minne lay. A fine architect was brought to design a building in a new style of truly Adirondack architecture far more compatible with wilderness surroundings than the Victorian structures one saw sticking up through the trees. The style wasn't actually entirely new since it combined the features of the indigenous log cabin of early days, which was a matter of expediency, with those of the Swiss chalet. Very wealthy men were buying up huge tracts of Adirondack wilderness lands. They had travelled extensively both here and abroad so the idea came about naturally. To the log cabin were added steep roofs, balconies and Swiss ornamentation done in Adirondack fashion. Probably the style was first used at William West Durant's famous Camp Pine Knot on Raquette Lake. Durant was the son of Dr. Thomas Durant who was in large part responsible for driving Union Pacific's tracks to Promontory Point in far away Utah. Pine Knot, built in 1876, became legendary, people travelled far for even a glimpse of it. Whether Cyrus Butler was ever a guest there I do not know but the hotel he built at Black Mountain certainly showed the camp's influence. Using the word 'sophisticated' in its truest sense the hotel might have been described as having sophisticated rusticity. The verandahs, eaves, cornices and balconies, even the stable, wore intricate patterns of "wooden lace" made of unpeeled cedar. This was the Adirondack adaptation of Swiss chalet ornamentation. Something resembling it was used in the gazebo at Shelving Rock Falls. The main building was of logs and siding. So compatible with the landscape was the style that Stoddard wrote in 1880: "It is the most striking and picturesque hotel on Lake George and worthy of the aesthetic taste of Cyrus Butler and (his) distinguished architect. It seems here a part of nature's self".

About this time the road from Caldwell to Bolton began to be known as "Millionaires' Row". While the estates were not nearly as large in over-all scope as those deeper in the Adirondack the homes themselves were mansions. Far from being rustic in style they resembled the fashionable trends of Saratoga complete with formal gardens, iron stags, marble statues, fountains, crystal chandeliers and mahogany.

Probably Butler's first consideration when chosing a name for the hotel honored the Horicon Iron Works which owned the land. He called it Horicon Pavilion. He must also have known however, that the name Horican went back further in the annals of the region. It might once have become the name of the lake itself. Years earlier James Fenimore Cooper claimed the existence of an old French map which located an Indian tribe, Les Horicanes, hereabouts. He consequently called the lake "Horicon" in his novels while agitating strenuously to have the name become the official one. While delicately suggesting that the name might have been applied first by his famous character, the scout Natty Bumpo, Cooper stated with some real justification that the Iroquois appelation of "Andiatarocte" was "unpronounceable," the French "Lac du St. Sacrament" too complicated, the American "George" "to commonplace" and after all honoring a Hanovarian king! His arguments can be read in the introduction to "Last of The Mohicans". Whatever the truth about the alleged map another famous figure of American literature years later was heard to remark a little acidly that "Coopers Indians were often an extinct tribe that never existed." Apparently the speaker, known best as Mark Twain, didn't have a high opinion of his predecessor's knowledge of Indians! Whether Sam Clemens was right or wrong the fact remains that the lake was not renamed after Sir William Johnson claimed it for his king. The name Horicon has however been used frequently in the area. Two of the lake's later great sidewheelers were so christened, one the Minne's immediate successor Horicon I. In the same guidebook in which Stoddard described the Minne's new role as a hotel he enthused about the new boat. Her length was all of 203 feet as against the Minne's 144. She was "of graceful poise and fast making 20 MPH!" Her 108 foot salon was elegantly panelled in native butternut and black walnut. From her snug bay at Black Mt. the Minne watched her pass daily, rocked gently in her swells and heard her deep voice bouncing off the familiar mountains. The Minne had become a floating annex of the Pavilion now, a most delightful place for young guests! They could play at being real steamboatmen aboard to their hearts' content. Probably many felt as did the youthful Mark Twain that to become a steamboatman would be the height of glorious adulthood.

Horicon Pavilion like the rebuilt Minne was designed as much for daytime visitors who wished to climb the mountain and find a good meal awaiting their return as for longer staying guests. The hotel had a large pleasant dining room but only twelve bedrooms. There was a stable full of horses and mules for those who wished to ride up the mountain or perhaps southward toward Shelving Rock over the level shore road the lumbermen left. A large old poster of the place survives bearing a drawing from the mountain top and a romantically worded account of the trail up. The view from the summit is of course extensive as no other in the area although other mountain tops nearby have each their own charm. From the top of Black the Adirondacks run tier on tier to the high peaks to the west, to the east lie the Green Mts. of Vermont, green then lavender and blue while a far more distant softer blue shows the outlines of the great White Mts. of New Hampshire. To the south can be seen the mighty valley of the Hudson while northward down the expanse of Lake Champlain the skyline of Montreal city can be seen on a clear day.

That old poster has this to say too; "On the mountain the scars of great fires are rapidly disappearing under brave new growth"! An insert reads as follows about the Pavilion itself:

> "Round table dinners of from ten to twenty can be ordered. In order to ensure the best decorum and promote the happiness of the majority especially of women and children and non-consumers there will not be sold or permitted on the premises wines, liquors, or beer. Lunch 50 cents, dinner or lodging $1, breakfast or supper 75 cents, per day $3. The Pavilion will remain open until November 1st."

According to all accounts Cyrus Butler, when present, was a very delightful host. Nor were his plans completed with the building of the Pavilion. Of course the needed steamboat landing was built, also providing a sheltered docking space for small craft. This pier extended out from a whalebacked rock south of Black Mt. Point. A rustic bridge led from rock to shore. The old path to it is one of the few things still traceable. Butler's own little steamer, The Meteor, was often berthed there, the same boat which had towed the Minne on her last trip down-lake. Next Butler planned to build a small camp on the mountain's summit so that guests could spend the night there and enjoy sunset and sunrise from so fine a vantage place. He also had in mind a cottage colony around the wide lawns before the Pavilion. The cottages would be rentable by week or season.

These further dreams and plans came to an abrupt end in 1889. In his guidebook of that spring Stoddard who had written so glowingly of the Pavilion's charm wrote a sort of valediction. "Horicon Pavilion at Black Mt. was destroyed by fire on April 21st . . . it was a poem in wood and stone." He did not say and perhaps did not know how the fire started. Most likely the place was being readied for opening, a faulty flue, an overheated stove or carelessness with lamp or candle might have started the blaze. In so isolated a place there was little could be done to save the structure.

Once again thereafter Stoddard wrote of Cyrus Butler, this time in his guide of 1893. He clearly showed his respect and admiration for the man and again it was a sort of valediction. Butler had hoped to form an artists colony on Meadow Point near Huletts but "the plans died with him. He was a friend and generous enthusiast to many a struggling artist and musician, his generosity limited only by his means." Butler had not long survived his beautiful Pavilion. Undoubtedly he was a man of many facets not least of which were geniality and a profound kindly interest in fellow human beings.

This then is the story of what is probably one of the least known of the earlier lake resorts. As for the Minne, she lay for a time in her snug bay below the charred ruins, a prey to ravages of wind and weather, and abandoned. It was finally deemed safest to dynamite her superstructure to avoid accidents to curious wayfarers for people still came to climb the mountain eagerly. Her hull sank in the bay where it lies today. The heavy iron rings which helped moor her are all that is left intact of Butler's venture. They remain firmly embedded in the ledge rock of Black Mt. Point.

In time the lands of the Horicon Iron Works passed into other hands. Lumbering along the lake became severely curtailed by law as the lake became more and more a recreation-resort area. The shoreline and mountains northward from Shelving Rock to a point beyond Black Mt. summit were eventually part of the large Knapp Estate, but the trail Butler had built up the mountain remained open to all at all times.

During the years from early in this century until 1941 when the Black Mt. area was part of the big estate a boys' camp was given usage of the locality where Horicon Pavilion had stood. The lawn, already overgrowing, was still clear enough however to make a fine playing field. Along the abandoned loop of road on which the hotel fronted a site for archery was laid out although a tangle of bittersweet vines had spread there rapidly. The last trail ever started for George Knapp through all his vast property ran northward from the road's ending toward Huletts which place it never reached. A little distance along it the camp built a place for Sunday worship. One might have called it a wilderness chapel for its pews were rough logs, its nave a carpet of pine needles, the arches overhead the branches of living trees. The sky was its ceiling. The duly consecrated altar was the only man-made thing, being constructed of stone and cement. This place too is hardly recognizable today for the ways of the forest are quicker than one might suppose. Logs decay, branches and trees fall. For some time after the camp was gone and the land became state-owned someone each year fashioned a rustic cross for the altar and kept it erect there. It was made of branches bound together with a wild grape vine. I do not know who he or she was or why it was done. For reasons of my own I liked to go there at least once each year and sometimes still do. One September not so very long ago there was no longer a cross. I had the feeling that a story had to come to an ending somewhere. I'd brought some bright leaves and wild asters as I usually did: On impulse I stayed long enough to wind together two branches with a wild grape vine which grew nearby.

I was intensely aware that day along the trail back to Black Mt. Point. It was very quiet, the season for picnickers over. Waves from my boat had long spent themselves having rolled like quicksilver to break on the shore. The calm lake wore the dulled burnishment of a very old mirror. In the sort of gentle sun-warmth which only September brings to the north country the grass under my feet sparkled with heavy dew. (Someone has spoken of grass as nature's forgiveness). Hundreds of tiny spider webbs were filagrees of dew damonds too.

An official state trail sign, yellow lettered on brown, pointed the way upward to deep forests, bare high ledges, a windswept summit, all on a trail built by a man named Butler almost a hundred years ago. Part of it was hacked out by lumbermen even longer before. Where I knew the Pavilion's wide lawn had been tall wheat colored grasses sheltered more and more seedlings of the eager forest. I wondered idly whether the grass had a way of knowing that those seedlings would one day draw the cycle again to completion?

There'd been no great timber coming down those slopes for years, horses, oxen, brawn and muscle doing the work not bulldozers, power saws and tractors. The time worn cry of the lumberjack, "TIMBER!", was long since stilled. The weatherbeaten house where those men rested aching backs, ate johnnycake and slept with noisy snores has disappeared without a trace. Hank Durrin's porcupine hides are a part of forest duff, the same forest which has all but swallowed what remained of Horicon Pavilion.

Once there had been dancing, music and laughter there but now I listened acutely to a different, older music. It was that of a suddenly rising wind. The leaves and needles began to talk. I didn't entirely understand the language, for no one can, but I felt there was reassurance in it. It was a song of inevitable seasonal change and timeless wonder. A stronger gust came with almost razor sharpness, summer's coda?

The wheaten grasses bent all one way and sighed. Leaves of birches came sailing down. They were flakes of gold but not the gold whose seeking can bring disaster. Some of the leaves reached the waters of the bay where the bones of an old steamboat rest. They floated there ever so delicately. Then the wind found them out and they were off again twisting and turning as if jockeying for place. Finally they seemed to be racing like tiny boats to some distant finish line.

As I started my own boat I was strongly aware once again that time and nature are many things to each of us. They build, destroy, they teach . . . and they can heal.

Perhaps Cyrus Butler once left this same spot with very similar thoughts.

Aerial view south over Paradise and Red Rock bays. Buck Mountain in distance, Shelving Rock on right.

Photo by Richard Dean

Launch in Paradise Bay.

French Point and its hotel from across the lake.

The Sherman House, French Point.   Stoddard Photo

Annex cottage at French Point.   Stoddard Photo

Hank Durrin and son Sherm.
Photo Courtesy of Mrs. Jesse Stiles

Durrin's bear cubs at Shelving Rock Falls. -- Photo Courtesy of Mrs. Jesse Stiles

Two details of woodwork on Shelving Rock Falls gazebo.   *Photo by the Author*

Cyrus Butler's "Meteor" tows the Minne to Black Mountain Point.

Horicon Pavilion at foot of Black Mountain.

Stoddard Photo

Horicon Pavilion and guests. *Photo from Lake George Camp and Canoe Chats*

Horicon Pavilion's steamer landing from hotel porch. *Stoddard Photo*

Rear entrance, Horicon Pavilion.   *Stoddard Photo*

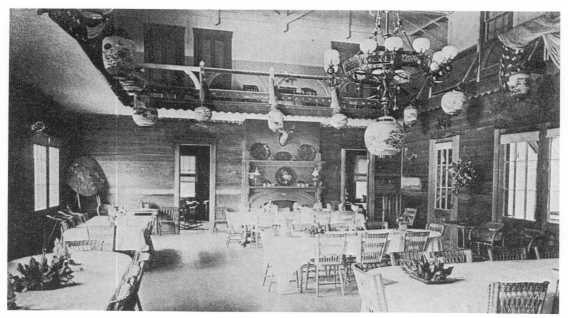

Dining room, Horicon Pavilion.   *Stoddard Photo*

Horicon Pavilion verandah showing woodwork. *Stoddard Photo*

The rebuilt Minne-Ha-Ha moored at Black Mountain Point below Horicon Pavilion. *Stoddard Photo*

Salon of the Minne-Ha-Ha at Black Mt.　　　　　　　　　　　　　　*Stoddard Photo*

Another view of the Minne's salon　　　　　　　　　　　　　　*Stoddard Photo*

142

The late veteran Lake George Captain Alanson Fisher and his son Captain Martin Fisher. Steamboating was often a way of life through several generations. This photo was taken aboard Champlain's Ticonderoga which the Fishers operated when the day of steam had ended on Lake George. The "Ti" is now at Shelburne Museum, Vt.

Photo Courtesy of Captain and Mrs. Martin Fisher

Hull of the Minne-Ha-Ha just before it sank at Black Mountain Point

First airplane on Lake George, 1913   *Photo Courtesy of the late Miss Helen Simpson*

Log cabin on branch of the Mountain Road destroyed by fire in the 1940s   *Photo by George R. Simon*

Red schoolhouse at Hogtown where later Herman Benton lived   *Photo Courtesy of Mrs. Jesse Stiles*

"*The Mountain Road*"
— *Painting by the Author*

Chapter 12

A Steamboat and A Child

The great white sidewheelers are gone from this lake. Their final demise came in 1938 when the last and largest of them all, Horicon II was towed out from the shipyards at Baldwin one windless evening and burned. It wasn't worth salvaging any of her, her usefulness was over. Quite a few people on seeing pictures of such boats ask incredulously whether there were really such vessels on the lake? The pictures manage to convey something of their elegance, their sparkling white hulls, their decks surmounted by a tall black stack which somehow resembled a thin, elongated stove pipe hat. The pictures cannot convey the excitement generated all along the lake's landings at steamboat time. The piers would be crowded with people, some just there for the flavor. Those who have missed seeing the boats never saw something closely related to the development of this country. Further, the steamboats left us more than the knowledge of their physical usefulness through the 19th century. The lake and river sidewheelers and sternwheelers also left a heritage of romance, ballads, folklore and song akin to that of the Santa Fe and Oregon trails and the empire building railroads which followed the Conestoga wagon. There was a sense of gallantry about those boats spiced with a certain devil-maycareness.

There follows an account of a trip on Horicon II seen through the eyes of a child. Quite a number of years ago a little girl stood on the pier at Shelving Rock Landing. Her eyes were dark with anticipation. This day a familiar event would nevertheless be different. She herself was soon to go aboard the 230 foot Horicon II and for the first time see the northern reaches of the lake. The child couldn't know that the boat was destined to be the last of a long, long line. Her climactic luxury saw the ending of an era and in a sense a way of life here. No one really grasped this at the time for such boats had served their grandparents.

To the child steamboat arrivals often meant the coming of her father or grandfather or uncle, it was the last leg of their journey from the city. It also might mean their departure again when it was hard to choke down tears for to a child a two week absence seems an eternity. Sometimes too there was freight arriving, barrels of coffee beans, flour, sugar, trunks or other things. The steamboat carried them all.

The little girl was in awe of those powerful paddle wheels, she'd often watched the foaming wake they sent streaming astern. It looked like the train of some regal lady sweeping on her way with great assurance. Her heart beat a little faster when the Horicon's big white bow appeared around Fourteen Mile Island to the south. Then the whistle sounded for the landing, a white puff of steam on the tall black stack showing where the whistle was located. One could hear the rhythm of the paddlewheels slowing and see a rush of activity on the forward main deck. Time wasn't to be wasted for the Horicon had a schedule to keep. There was a high pitched squealing as the boat's heavy guards met the pier's fenders, wood protesting against wood. Briefly the paddlewheels reversed their turning and then stopped with cascades of water streaming from the buckets. Huge hawsers now strained at the dock posts and young deck hands leapt ashore dragging the heavy gangplank used for freight. Mail and freight carts rattled down it onto the pier to be unloaded with dispatch. Passengers crowded the starboard rails of the deck above to observe and be observed by those ashore.

Way up on the hurricane deck gay flags fluttered for it was company policy to "dress ship" with flags of several nations.

"Come along now", said the little girl's mother, taking the small hand. They went up the slightly bouncy gangplank and the child kept her eyes away from those paddlewheels which were now so close. She didn't look down at the water either for it was still so angry from their churning.

Aboard a brand new world awaited, beyond anything in her previous experience. There was even a new smell, indigenous to the steamboats always. It was a composite of swabbed decks, brass polish, all manner of freight, leather trunks, luncheon being prepared for hungry travellers, all bound up in the overall, one might say catalytic smell of steam.

The gangplank rattled back aboard, bells rang somewhere and then there began underfoot a sensation like the beating of a giant pulse. It was slow at first and then faster and faster as the Horicon was on her way again.

"We'll buy our tickets now," mother directed, "then if you like we'll have lunch in the dining salon while we are still in a part of the lake you know well." Halfway aft to the purser's office the child stopped open-mouthed. The pulsating took on reason. Through large glass windows the stroking of Horicon's huge connecting rod could be seen along with the glittering polished steel and brass of the piston rod, both seemingly within arm's length. One could look down too into the ship's belly, a mysterious place of all sorts of brightly polished brass gauges and other strange things.

Even at her rather tender age the child surmised that the enormous rod drove those paddlewheels in some manner. How it did this she couldn't figure out (and still can't exactly). But she knew also that the piles of black coal on the pier at Caldwell and ordinary lake water produced steam which activated all this. There was another curious bit of the boat's machinery she'd often watched from shore. Her parents said it was a "walking beam", a huge iron triangular affair which see-sawed back and forth above the topmost (hurricane) deck. Perhaps this was the connecting link, she thought, between what went on inside the ship and the paddlewheels?

Suddenly as she gazed down through the big window the boat's engineer popped up a vertical ladder like a genie from the underworld who wanted to take a quick look topside. The little girl smiled timidly at him and he grinned back broadly before disappearing back into the regions below. It's a different sort of world I'm in, thought the youngster, but the people in it are awfully nice.

As they walked astern they came to a set of steps up and over a wide hump in the main deck.

"What's this for, mother?"

"You're climbing over the big shaft that runs out to turn the paddlewheels," her mother replied having done her homework well.

"Oh!", said her daughter and scurried across for this meant the dangerous wheels were awfully close by. Her feelings about them stemmed from very frequent warnings all children were given to keep rowboats and canoes well away from the steamboats. The giant paddlewheels created a strong suction.

Luncheon was a treat by itself. Eating on a steamboat while watching the shores and islands seem to slide by was even better than eating in a restaurant. White linen and silver plate adorned the wide tables and waiters served with friendly deftness.

As they went up on deck a little later the Horicon was sounding her imperious voice for Huletts Landing tucked behind old Cap'n Harris's Elephant Mountain. The child leaned over the rail as other passengers did to stare at the crowd on the pier and the cottages and hotels along shore. She felt rather sophisticated when she noticed children down there gaping up at the boat as she had always done.

"Now we cross the lake to Sabbath Day Point," mother informed her. "It's said the first house was built there in the 1760s! There's a passable road to there from Ticonderoga up north but I understand there's talk of connecting it with the Bolton Road and making a real highway of it from one end of the lake to the other."

"Isn't there any road over Tongue Mt?" asked the little girl.

"Yes," mother answered, "But it's pretty much the terribly steep narrow old military road built by the French in French and Indian War days. It's very bad and few people use it. That's why the steamboats carry all the mail and freight and travellers up and down the lake."

"But why do they need a highway?" asked the child. "I think a steamboat is much more fun than a silly road. One can go on a road anytime!"

"I 'spose because so many people are buying automobiles these days," her

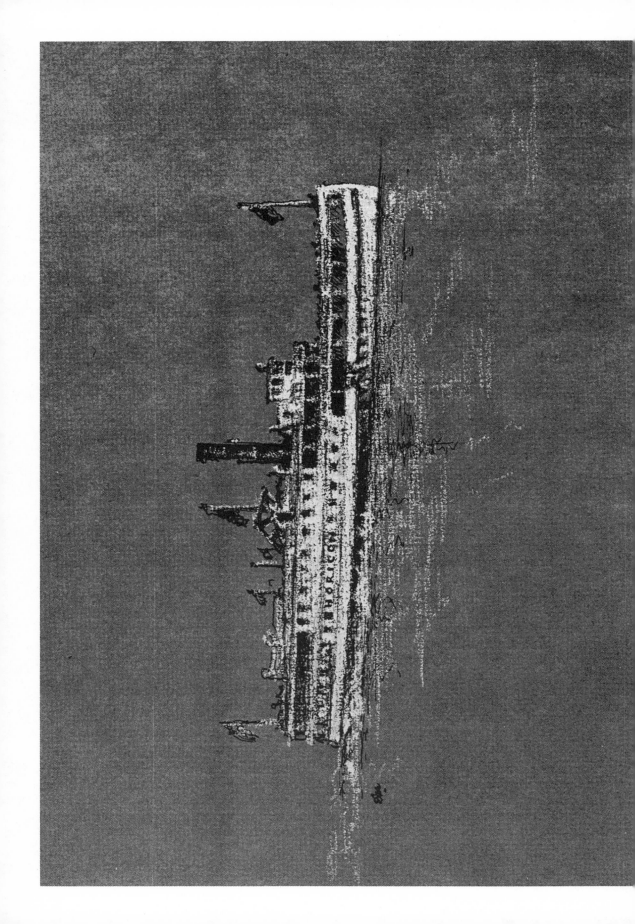

parent replied. "People can get places faster in a car."

Even mother couldn't know how soon the gasoline engine would bring about vast changes.

"I wonder why they want to go fast and not see anything on the way?" The little girl shook her head then asked, "Why is it called Sabbath Day Point?"

"It isn't really known who called it that first. It was a favorite camping place for armies and scouting parties during the colonial wars. Some historys say a British general named Amherst let his soldiers rest there over the Sabbath before attacking the French at Ticonderoga but others say the place had the name much earlier."

The child was silent for a time. Suddenly she asked,

"Mother, why are there wars? Why do men want to kill each other, 'specially if they don't even know each other?"

The mother looked away over the sparkling sunlit water and the green and purple mountains. In her heart and mind she heard the thundering guns of World War I just ended. She could formulate no adequate answer and knew the child's attention would soon be on something else. And she was right. Her daughter was trying to visualize a whole army on that pretty point with swords and muskets and cannon and martial music . . . and Indian allies! She'd seen pictures of scarlet coats, and bewigged officers, of Scottish tartans and bagpipes and painted Indian warriors. But they seemed incongruous figures ever to have been on that lovely point.

Horicon's whistle sounded again and again as the boat swung into landings where gay crowds awaited her. Then there was the rush and hurry below on the main deck for Horicon had a rendevouz to keep with a waiting train.

Roger's Rock loomed into sight, that cliff-faced mountain named after the famous scout and ranger of French and Indian War days. The little girl begged to hear the story once more about the man and the mountain.

"I'll bet Major Rogers knew all about the lake and the woods the way John Stiles does, didn't he, mother?" Here was an historical figure the child could better understand. "Men like that don't ever get scared, they know just what to do always don't they?"

Mother smiled a little. "I wouldn't be so sure of that," she said. "The major had lots of enemy Indians looking for him and they were pretty smart too. He had lots of courage, and so does John, but that doesn't mean one isn't afraid sometimes and uncertain. One does what one has to do in spite of it. That's where courage comes in!"

"Major Rogers was a resourceful man just like John," mother went on. "He certainly knew his way about the woods and lake. The Indians who sided with the French considered him an arch-enemy and one winter day they thought they had him cornered on that mountain. They knew it had a sheer cliff on the lake side. The major got to the top of the cliff and quickly made a decision. He unbuckled his pack and let it slide down the rock face onto the ice. Then he put his snowshoes on backwards and retraced his own trail to a ravine which he descended. When the Indians, fooled by a single track got to the cliff they saw the scuff marks made by the pack and their enemy way down below on the lake. They thought he'd gone down the terrible cliff himself and so must be a super-human or some kind of devil. It was best to leave such a one be! And so Major Rogers escaped."

The little girl's eyes shone. "John Stiles would be just as smart I think if he didn't want to get caught!" she said loyally.

"It's entirely possible," mother laughed. The child looked up at the great rock face and almost thought she could see Indians up there. It was exciting to think so anyway. After landing below the lovely white columned Rogers Rock Hotel the Horicon headed for the northern terminal landing at Baldwin. The place was named after the Captain Baldwin who years earlier had operated a stage line between Lakes George and Champlain. The whistle sounded a prolonged blast as the steamer swung in a great arc so that her bow would be pointing southward at landing. The paddlewheels churned up mud and sand in the rapidly shallowing water until it looked like cafe au lait. The lake was narrowing sharply toward its outlet and the great mills of Ticonderoga downstream.

At the pier a small edition of a train awaited northbound travellers. It was panting and puffing so much one could almost imagine its wheels were pawing at the tracks like a nervous horse anxious to be off. The child watched the passengers come and go and eyed the two silver ribbons of track wistfully. She wondered where they led. However the Horicon's voice soon announced the southbound departure. About an hour later the familiar Shelving Rock landing came into view after the last long unbroken run up the narrows.

When they landed there was no freight for shore so the smaller gangplank was used. It bounced and wobbled over the abyss between boat and pier in a fashion which made one feel like a low speed projectile about to be launched into space.

For mother and daughter the wonderous voyage was over. The child turned impulsively to wave at the boat. The captain himself returned her wave from the flying bridge. She wanted to watch as the Horicon's great white stern grew smaller and the frothing wake dissolved around the pier. She watched until the boat disappeared from sight around Fourteen Mile Island. Some years later she watched the great steamboat disappear into a place called history.

Steamboats did remain a part of life on the lake for some years after the little girl reached young adulthood. Shortly after the voyage just described she would cross the ocean on a great Atlantic liner but the trip on Horicon II would remain a special memory. True enough no whales had spouted as in the Atlantic, no porpoises raced alongside, there was no mysterious phosphorescence of a Gulf Stream or the boundless vastness of the sea. There was however a distinct essence of America a-building, something inherent in the sidewheeler Horicon which was symbolic of all the great rivers and lakes of the land as they became pathways beyond the frontiers.

The sidewheelers had a feature common to all lake and river paddleboats as well as canal barges. One turned the wheel to port in order to go to starboard and vice versa. This facilitated landings for the helmsman but it gave one barge captain in local waters some bad moments. Captain Orrin Belden of Ft. Ann decided to buy himself one of the new fangled automobiles. It was a model A Ford. The good captain set out cheerfully but the steering just didn't come naturally. He kept turning the wheel as he did that on his boat. He landed against a stone wall. Finally some kindly or perhaps apprehensive mechanic reversed the car's steering mechanism (which was quite possible to do on that model) and all went well thereafter. The roads were safer for neighbors too.

The same little girl who made that voyage on Hoicon II was several times given the pleasure, when grown up, of taking the wheel on lake steamboats for short stretches. The first occasion was aboard the Sagamore, sister ship of the Horicon. She was not aware of the difference in the steering. As she turned the wheel the big white bow swung majestically in the wrong direction. It was of course a wide open stretch of water ahead and she soon found out what to do but the captain, with a twinkle in his eyes informed her that the engineer had sent up a message asking why the boat was using twice the coal on that crossing? The wake of the Sagamore did indeed resemble a snake for a short spell. Her course had been anything but straight!

The last great sidewheeler hereabout operated on Lake Champlain until 1953. She was the "Ticonderoga", launched at Shelburne Harbor in 1906. Great efforts were made to keep her in service. They were made in part by two former Lake George steamboatmen, veteran Captain Alanson Fisher and his son Captain Martin Fisher. However the era of steamboats had ended, there were few left who understood the great steam engines and could serve as engineer. Even under the eventual auspices of the famous Shelburne Museum of Vermont operation became impractical. The boat faced the same fate all her kin had met earlier. She was to be scrapped. Fortunately this did not happen. The old "Ti" was hauled on specially laid tracks from Shelburne Harbor to the grounds of the Museum. She rests there today, a fine memorial to all her proud ancestry.

Almost all children taken to see the Museum today beg their parents "Oh please, can we go see that big wonderful white boat first of all?"

That wonderful white boat wears a placque on her bulkhead which designates her a National Historic Landmark.

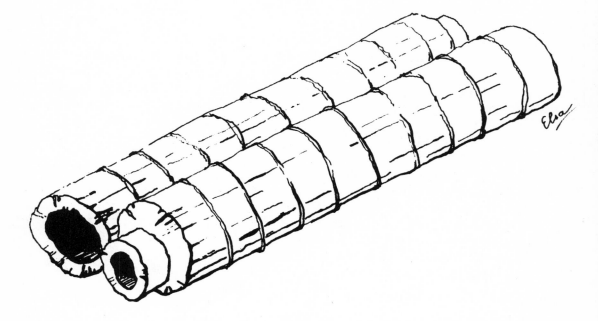

Wood water pipes probably used at old lumber mill atop Shelving Rock Falls. The wood strip pipes were tarred, rolled in sawdust and bound 'round with wire.

Chapter 13

The Mountain Road

The mountain road, specifically the one which climbs over the ridges and drops down to the lake at Shelving Rock hasn't changed its ways much during the century and more of its existence. Probably every mountainous area has a road known best by this simple, descriptive name. When such roads have an official one and a person uses it most people round about stare and ask. "What road would you be referring to?" Our mountain road is no exception. It had its beginning back in the earlier years of the 19th century as merely deepening wagon ruts which penetrated higher and further to where tall timber grew. It became a road through usage and nothing else. Of a certainty, no engineer laid out its course, its winds, climbs and twists its way around swamps, over ledges it can't avoid, and along and over brooks. Sometimes it squeezes its way along the eyebrow of a hill or descends a ravine with the abandon of a waterfall. In short it has that precious quality, individuality!

Perhaps quite naturally it instilled this quality into those who shaped it into what it is, even into the present century. Hogtown lies near the road's apex. For some years in the 1930s that deserted spot once again had inhabitants inured to old time ways. There were two of them. Both men were well on in years, each had chosen the place for reasons of his own. One was a hunter and mountain man from birth, brother to Lucinda White. This was Herman Benton, the same who helped Jack Dacy build the road to the summit of Shelving Rock years earlier. Herman looked over the long abandoned little red schoolhouse at "the corners". It fulfilled all his desires. Even the old privy out back still stood at a reasonably upright angle He forthwith nailed a pair of antlers over the schoolhouse door and moved in. He was a man of rather taciturn expression which often indicates someone not given to loquacity. This however was not the case with Herman. Although he'd never left the area he read endless novels which jelled into a flow of tales of personal experiences the world over, tales which emerged in all their imaginative glory when the audience seemed proper.

If Herman was indeed a character so was his neighbor across the road. Whence or why "Old Al" came to Hogtown no one ever really knew. It was a matter for all sorts of speculations, none ever verified. He was a small rather wrinkled and friendly man who took up residence in Hogtown for quite some years. Rather remarkable was the domicile he built himself just north of the old church. Al hauled in every board he came across and used it in the structure with no regard for length or breadth. The ultimate result resembled an old cartoon called "The Toonerville Trolley" complete with the crooked stove pipe which emerged through the roof. The

Old Al's domicile at Hogtown.

156

unique angles of the house would have driven an architect mad but it stood through storm and heavy snows year after year. The few who ever got inside were met by a wild flurry of chickens circling in alarm from their roosts on the rafters. Along with the birds Al shared his quarters with a goat. The floor had a carpet whose redeeming feature was layer on layer of wood shavings since Al spent his evenings whittling kindling for his stove!

In the early years of Al's residence in Hogtown he kept a horse and buggy. The story which follows is exactly as it was told to me.

"Now old Al was somewhat afraid of that nag. The beast was too lively or maybe he just waren't used to horses much. Anyways Al hit on an idea one day to slow the nag down. He waren't lookin' to end bottom side up in a ditch. He went out and cut a stout pole, trimmed it even and rammed it crosswise through the spokes of the buggy's hind wheels. He figgered this would be a sort of brake 'cause them back wheels 'ud be kept from turnin'. Then he got aboard and started. But that nag started off like he always done and the gol darn pole knocked every spoke outta them hind wheels straight off and the ass-end of the buggy hit the ground with a God-A-'mighty bang — and so did Al's!"

In later years Al depended on passers-by to hitch a ride to town or bring provisions to him. He was still, however, not without wiles on occasion! One winter night when the temperature hovered around -20° Ernest Granger was driving out from Shelving Rock to Ft. Ann. On the high level stretch known as Hogtown Flat he found a tree across the road. Examination showed the tree hadn't fallen of its own accord. While Ernest was removing it Al appeared out of the darkness. He admitted he'd dropped the tree there to halt the first passerby but he had good reason. He'd an order from Ft. Ann for some of his hens. Ernest good naturedly agreed to the passengers. Arrived at Al's shack he pulled up and waited. Al went in and hauled a crate from under his bunk which he put in the truck. The major business came next. The roused hens weren't easy to catch. One by one Al chased, caught and carried them to the crate. At last, clad only in a thin suit Al sat himself atop the crate and rode there all the freezing miles to town refusing to join Ernest in the cab. Perhaps he thought a hen or two might escape.

Those hens, incidentally, were destined for the first restaurant run by Beatrice Owens whose famous Hogtown Ranch would open some years later in 1952. Bea came by her love for the Hogtown area quite naturally. Her parents were Lucinda and Will White, her uncle, Herman Benton.

As for old Al, he became known as the Hermit of Hogtown although his predilection for visiting as long as anyone wanted to talk belied the usual concept of a hermit as was also the case with the famous Noah Rondeau of the Adirondacks. What Herman and Al talked about during the long stillnesses of the mountains in off seasons, or whether they talked much at all I do not know. At least they could see each other's smoke rising and dim light at night.

Al finally departed into the same obscurity out of which he had come and eventually his house tumbled down. Herman died a little later leaving his faithful companion a little dog named Soapy to the care of his sister Lucinda. When Soapy went to join her master Lucinda went to her brother's grave one dark night and buried the little dog beside him. "T'was in a cemetery and could be some folks 'ud say t'waren't right," she said, "But I done it anyway. Them two belonged together!" Remember, Lucinda too had been born along the mountain road!

To return to the road itself, quite possibly part of its route was once an Indian trail used in passage from the waterway of Lake George to the southern tip of Champlain's South Bay which lies just east of Shelving Rock. The road has less economic importance today than 70 or more years ago since it runs well away from the present mainstreams of traffic and industry. Lumber interests and farms which long needed it are gone like last summer's leaves. Traces remain to show of their existence, a cellar hole, a clearing, a row of huge maples, the skeletons of old apple trees almost lost in the density and darkness, now only mute evidences of the back-breaking toil of bygone generations.

Years ago, as the road lengthened, arms of it ravelled out like strands of yarn. These side roads and trails each had purposeful destinations. They followed brook valleys or ridges to isolated lumbermen's cabins or farms, they obeyed the will of the land, did not try to bend it as roads do today. The land was the boss and along the mountain road it still is. This does not produce monotony. The network of tributaries to the main stem will take one surprisingly far, to regions where today it is possible to get lost in uncertainty, to where a sense of direction can disappear, or where just possibly one can find a better one . . . !

Loving such a road means knowing what lies back of its physical course, not obvious things like mountains and valleys, streams and lakes but a form of landmark close to what Henry Thoreau found at Walden Pond and John Muir in the high Sierra where he often shouted out his joy aloud at the finding.

Such landmarks aren't exactly tangible but they nevertheless lie in pools along a brook where water reflects the sky and earth and even permits a look down into itself . . . a triple vision. Of course brooks accompany the mountain road, they had determined the best route long before the road was born. Such landmarks lie in the petals of a wildflower, in the matchless scent of arbutus when winter is barely gone, in the smell of burnished gold and copper ferns crisping in fall's first chill, in the exquisite combination of wind and falling leaf when summer's done. They're found in the green-blue ice which makes a waterfall in winter a thing of fantastic sculpture.

One sees such landmarks in the marvelous structure of tiny northern orchids scattered unobtrusively in the wild growth of old fields. They are hardly recognizable as of such a proud family, proud for orchids rank high in the scale of plant evolution. The overgrown old fields have an essence of their own as sharp and unmistakable as that of needles on the forest floor warmed by the sun. There's the richness of spring and summer, the choking splendor of autumn, the magnificent austere silence of winter that holds all in safekeeping for a time. These landmarks can guide one to immeasurable distances, as far as one wants to go . . .

More literally speaking the road watched man and earth working together with man respecting in full measure what the good earth provides. It saw the careful husbandry of acres such as those which produced Dacy's famous potatoes, it saw the planting and care of orchards where apples grew whose names are now almost forgotten but each of which had a special taste and usage. The names of these are like lines of verse. There were Spies and Russets, Talman, Pound, and Honey Sweets, Baldwins and Snows, Pignoses and Greenings, Wolf Rivers and Dutchesses, Gilliflowers and Seek-No-Furthers and Crabs. Some were for winter storage, some for harvest pies, jellies and cider, some would be dried or canned.

One strand of the road remembers until recently a log cabin farmhouse akin to those built in all frontier country. It had a single room under a tiny attic, the roof steeply pitched to shed heavy snows. The farm's once broad cleared acres are traceable still by the inevitable stone walls. Building those walls was backbreaking work but made the land easier for the plow, or at least a little more so, for stones almost seemed to sprout anew after each winter. Anyone who has ever handled a horse drawn plow will know what it felt like when the blades met a large stone beneath the surface! The jolt could be painful indeed.

Near a wall not far from the cabin site I once discovered a pile of broken "elixir" bottles. The imprinting in the glass promised a cure for most any ailment of man or beast. The cabin must have held a well stocked shelf since medical aid was far, far away especially in winter. There must have been too a jar of pine pitch from a chosen pitch tree for the substance was applied to festering sores or embedded splinters to draw out infection. Folks swore also to the efficacy of a spider web to stop a bleeding, of sweet flag root for an ailing stomach, of catnip tea to soothe a cold or quiet a teething baby, of countless other herbs and roots like ginseng for this or that complaint. Nature provided many wild things which had to be gathered at the proper time, dried, steeped or otherwise prepared. Necessities like soap were homemade products too. Soap was made from lye leached from wood ashes and fat rendered from animals. It may not have been so delicately perfumed but it got things clean!

The north country provided its sweeteners too in place of beet or cane sugar. The native sugar maples were the source of syrup and sugar. The boiling down was a late winter and early spring occupation. There was also wild honey to be gathered later on. Many an old timer made himself a bee-box for the purpose, a small receptacle with a sliding cover which was the means of tracing wild honey bees to their nests. Since these bees often range over an area of several miles the bee hunter needed time and patience. A bit of maple sugar or the like was put into the box sometimes covered with anise, a flavor greatly loved by bees. A wild bee would scent this in the open box, enter and be allowed to satiate itself when caught then depart for home when the lid opened again. The hunter would note the direction and follow. Arrived at the nest other bees would scent the delicious odor on their fellow worker or communicate knowledge in a strange dance. They would zero in on the bee box each one guiding the hunter on a truer course to the nest. At last he would be led to the hollow tree or cave which held it. Aside from the honey the nest provided beeswax which had a variety of uses. Candles were made of it and polishes. It was also used to wax thread such as that used by a shoemaker.

The old log cabin a ways off the mountain road was carefully preserved while the Knapp family owned the land on which it stood. It has since burned. Only the large rough stone that was a doorstep and the depression of a tiny cellar are left. It is said that twenty-three children were born to one mother in that cabin, she having married three times. The older ones were undoubtedly gone to "work out" when the younger ones came along. The children slept in the attic whose size couldn't have accommodated too many at a time.

A branch of the mountain road followed along the brook to the little lumber mill at Shelving Rock Falls. Stoddard often mentioned the site as "the lonely little clearing seen from lake steamers." The mill dam, still there but now built of stone

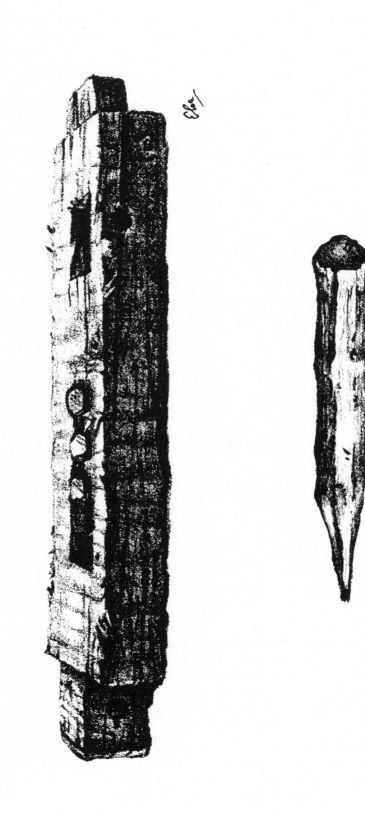

Old peg timber and oaken peg used.

and cement, was originally constructed of enormous logs. The mill and the miller's house are gone and probably the barn, the same in which Hank Durrin kept his bears, will soon follow them. Its magnificent hand hewn beams are a beautiful silver-grey with age, its forged iron hinges haven't allowed the doors to sag at all.*

All along its course the mountain road swings in arcs worn into rhythmic poetry. The banks are crowded close by ferns and mosses, grasses and wildflowers, lichens and fungi and the ever eager forest. The road's crown may injure an oil pan or knock off a muffler on occasion today. Some of the larger stones have been removed, this is true, adamant ledges receive fill once in a while. But the will of water hasn't changed so that storms wash man's efforts away, trees fall in whatever direction the power of wind or gravity ordains. The course of the mountain road remains close to nature's original structuralization.

Beavers often live near the road, building their remarkable way of life on the brooks, flooding old meadowlands in some places. Their engineering skill is certainly comparable to that of the road's while their determination is almost undefeatable. Deer, raccoons, bears, porcupines, skunks, rabbits, bobcats, and scores of lesser fry pay little attention to the unobtrusive man-way although they take care to avoid the unpredictable two legged creatures who use it and with whom they have no quarrel. Birds bathe in the road's dust even owls whose soft feathered wings permit them to fly so silently.

On the lakeward slopes the farms are all gone. Much of the land, for many recent years a part of the Knapp property, now belongs to the state. Some of the old farm houses and their outbuildings are so long gone no one living can recall exactly where they stood. The foundations of others are still marked by clumps of orange lilies, a lilac bush, or a rose. Wild things are taking back their own along the mountain road and this in itself couldn't be called sad, it is nature's timeless way. Economic conditions have changed as regards small farms, they can no longer exist profitably. What would be sad, and sometimes already is, would be the diminution of self reliance, ingenuity, and creativity which were once the requirements of daily life. These qualities bred a strong people. Earlier days left a heritage of this strength which should not be forgotten or ignored even in the telling of them. Certainly much has been made faster, vaster and easier by increased power of mechanization but this exacts a price in more ways than one, too. Given all the sundry benefits of machines they nevertheless often tend to standardize both product and producer losing somewhere along the line an independent pride of achievement. Something might seem throttled of the vital human qualities mentioned above. History often enough has shown that too little demand on individual ingenuity and self-reliance can lead to decadence and eventual disaster.

Still and all there will always, hopefully, be those who need a frontier to explore wherever or whatever it may be. They would be restless without a challenge to meet, a mountain top to reach so that life would not become meaningless. A frontier belongs to individualism and its utmost capabilities. This remains as true as the indomitable will of wild things to take back their own along the mountain road and elsewhere.

The road gained its sweeping grace, its beauty, through usage, its rhythm and

---

* On demolition in 1974 the skeletal structure of that barn revealed beams and timbering put together with whittled wooden pegs about 8" long tapered to a sharp point. The nails were hand forged square ones and adz marks were clearly visible on enormous beams measuring up to 30 ft. in length, all attesting to the age of the structure.

poetry through the vicissitudes of time, a knowledge of sun and storm. As to our road's beginning and ending points, if anything can be said to have a beginning and an ending, it is of no matter really. What does matter is that such by-roads still exist roaming over the hills and valleys of the land. What lies along the way of these, without the pressures and hurry of modern highways, is still a frontier in its own way in that which lies eternally waiting for unhurried perception the while giving much to the perceptive as each sees it in his own way.

Such roads lead to something "over the ridges" we cannot afford to lose. It's as though they spoke with their own voices saying "keep coming home, America, to the things that made you great".

Chapter 14

By Those Inaudible Words

By about mid-April the ice is generally gone from the lake. In spite of Cap'n Harris it hasn't sunk to the bottom to confound fishermen. Far more prosaically it has simply melted in warming temperatures. Of course the break-up varies considerably according to the nature of the season. Trees are more often than not still bare of leaf, snow loiters in patches in the woods or on northern slopes while dirt roads become mud roads for a time with some seemingly bottomless holes. The climax of the thaw consequently has become known as "mud week". Things are stirring though. The big sugar maples are often about done giving of their sweet sap to syrup and sugar makers if temperatures have levelled off for then the sap no longer runs from roots to crown and back again morning and night. Green spikes have begun to appear out of the earth with inate courage. They are as yet hardly recognizable as any specific plant except to an expert but the very sight of them is enough. In the fields the tall grasses of autumn's maturity which were flattened by a blanket of snow for so long lift their sered heads a little as the new grass pushes up from below.

It's an old custom along the lake to place bets as to the exact date on which the lake will be open water again. A fine point arises sometimes as to whether a few floating icecakes count or not. Each wager is based on inherited ken or private obstruse reasoning but whatever the case it's a day to mark on the calendar when the steely ice once more becomes sparkling water. Suddenly spring is closer, not as set by the calculated date of the vernal equinox but by a feeling in one's bones!

Sometimes the ice breaks into miniature icebergs of considerable thickness and heft. Shoved by a high wind these can cause havoc along shore crushing, grinding and dislodging man made things as well as nature's. If the ice melts slowly it often comes to resemble a honeycomb. Walking along shore beside it there's a whispering and tinkling as it stirs like the music of some strange instrument.

A little later spring shows other signs, the stern aloof blue mountains find traces of delicate green or pale pink about their feet, colors which in infinite variations wash slowly up to the summits, valley by valley, ledge by ledge, until the sternness is gone and the slopes look young and soft and joyful. The green enigmas of the forest floor have become entities now. Some turn out to be the illusive wild flowers of the north country, hepatica, trillium, bloodroot, wild ginger, violets, Dutchman's breeches, anemone and hosts of others. Last year's arbutus leaves, tough and leathery, still partially protect the pearly, incomparable blossoms in their midst. Ferns unfold almost as one watches, the fiddle-necked tips of some of them considered tastier than early asparagus!

Then one evening a symphony begins in the swamps and ponds. The tiny, one inch frogs known as peepers have descended out of the forest to invade the water and deposit their eggs, for frogs begin life as tadpoles, not amphibians. The symphony becomes actually stereophonic when the larger frogs join the treble of the peepers. the basso of the bull frog adds the final touch!

Migratory birds return, blackbirds, sparrows, tanagers, finches, vireos, warblers, whipporwills and more. The wild Canada geese in great V's continue to their nesting grounds in the far north. Their voices from out of the sky can never be mistaken for any other once heard. The sound somehow epitomizes the freedom of all wilderness. Once more one hears the matchless songs of the thrushes, Woodthrush, robin, bluebird and veery. If one is lucky there can be moments of magic, usually deep in the woods, where the hermit thrush, perhaps the finest song-bird in the world, chooses to nest. The magnificent song of this bird, ascending and descending the scale, holds within it the sheerest witchery of the deep forest.

Brooks become really ecstatic. There is pure exhileration in the leaping joy of white water. Fishermen and white water canoeists are equally ecstatic, once more in a kingdom far beyond the concept of ordinary mortals.

Full summer is green and blue, the shades changing from hour to hour, moment to moment. Most visitors know the lake best in this season.

Somewhere in September there comes an almost indefinable change, little things foretell what's ahead. Birches become golden and in the swamps a maple here and there turns such a crimson as is almost imcomprehensible. Late goldenrods and star-like clusters of wild asters fill the fields and open woodlands, and then slowly and with consummate majesty the magnificence of the northern fall paints the mountains and shores and islands reaching a climax by mid-October whose transience is exquisitely necessary. One couldn't stand to live long with so much glory!

Indian Pipes

Then the leaves fall, their work done. The wild geese return from the north pausing sometimes in their arrow flights to rest and feed on the lake before winging on. How they and other birds set their courses no one as yet really knows. Once more the mountains now wrap themselves in a remoteness that is deep blue.

Winter can come most silently if it chooses for snow makes no noise when it falls. It lays a cold, impartial blanket over everything, softening contours or erasing them completely. Mid to end January finds the lake once more locked in ice but while it then seems rigid and motionless and silent this is hardly true. Expansion and contraction take place, cracks open up and great pressure ridges form, aided and abetted by currents and fluctuating temperatures. As when a branch breaks with a crack like a pistol shot on a very cold night so the lake speaks in winter when the ice moves. The voice is a hollow, almost unearthly sound which seems to have no specific starting and ending point and reverberates like thunder. It can be heard far back from shore! It can scare the devil out of the uninitiated who happen to be on the ice itself! People listen and say "The lake is booming . . .".

1918 saw the closing of the last hotel in the narrows region. An era was ending. Pearl Point alone had existed well into its twilight. Those old resorts were part of a less hurried, less restless day. True enough they had what we might term great inconveniences today as regarded not only time and energy in reaching them but also in the deluxe accommodations required today. Nevertheless the advantages of 20 century living are not without serious drawbacks. Aside from the pressures of speed are such things as over-commercialization, vastly increased littering and the dangers inherent in careless pollution.

Fortunately many people still know the value of physical exertion in reaching a desired goal. They know too that the acceleration of daily living in the modern world needs the deceleration, renewal and peace which are found in wilderness places. They know how much there is to be said for the preservation of quiet bays, mountain solitudes and wild rivers and lakes. The feel of the good earth under one's feet, under one's own power, the feel of a paddle blade or oar, the billowing of a sail, these are still inestimably revitalizing experiences.

Whatever the pros and cons may seem to be as regards life then and now I personally am thankful that from earliest childhood I have known a canoe and its magic. Man-made it most certainly is, but semi-wild it is also! No craft is more an age old proven companion of wilderness. A canoe can move in exquisite silence sensitive to the slightest current or wind or twist of the wrist. It is also capable of great feats of endurance and strength. Like the shadow of a cloud it can reach secret places little else can know save the wild ones which live there or come to feed in the shallows. Reeds, grasses and water lilies sway aside unhurt by that gentle bow since a canoe floats with the lightness of a newly fallen leaf or the feather of a bird.

I have also had the privilege of growing up with the knowledge of mountain tops. There's something which draws one upward and upward 'til there's only sky above, deep blue or dotted with marching clouds or mists that have always seemed to me to move with the majesty of symphonic music, a mighty symphony! From such a place in early morning the other mountains stand soft lavender and always softer in receding tiers to the west. To the east the sun can as yet send only bright shafts through the high notches and the slopes below are deep purple or dark blue-green. Suddenly here and there high moist ledges sparkle like diamond tiaras as his solar majesty climbs a little higher. Up there one has a feeling of being very close (as did

Old Mountain Phelps) to something exquisitely rare in human experience.

The fact has remained constant even today that the lake and mountains are at their finest to one who comes quietly, to the oarsman, canoeist or skater, or to one afoot on a trail be it walking, skiing or on snowshoes. Such ones learn in the sincerity of their coming a reaffirmation of truths which are both beautiful and vital. Hearing and vision become sharpened and tuned to understand with a sort of empirical clarity much which relates deeply to the bases of life and living, and perhaps even of what we term death. It would indeed seems that something very wonderful is present, most assuredly so, in the ageless cycles of sun and storm, soil, rock, forest and field, stream and lake and the indomitable life there-in. It is even audible, if one listens acutely, in so slight a sound as that of a pine needle falling as a new needle takes its place.

Bibliography

Bird, Harrison; NAVIES IN THE MOUNTAINS
Bland, John; THE FORESTS OF LILLIPUT (Realm of Mosses & Lichens)
Bryant, William Cullen (edited by); PICTURESQUE AMERICA; 1872
Butler, E.C.; LAKE GEORGE AND LAKE CHAMPLAIN; 1869
Carmer, Carl; THE HUDSON
Carmer, Carl; LISTEN FOR A LONESOME DRUM
Carpenter, W.S.; SUMMER PARADISE IN HISTORY; 1914
Cole, G.G. (Editor); NORTH COUNTRY LIFE
Cooper, J.F.; LAST OF THE MOHICANS; 1826
D & H Press; THE STEAMBOATS OF LAKE CHAMPLAIN
D & H Press; THE STEAMBOATS OF LAKE GEORGE
DeCosta, B.F.; LAKE GEORGE; 1868
DeSormo, Maitland; SENECA RAY STODDARD pamphlet and book
Donaldson, Alfred; HISTORY OF THE ADIRONDACKS; 1921
Harris, Elias; LAKE GEORGE, ALL ABOUT IT; 1903
Hill, Ralph Nading; SIDEWHEELER SAGA
Holden, Dr. A.W.; HISTORY OF THE TOWN OF QUEENSBURY; 1874
HISTORY OF WARREN COUNTY; 1965
HISTORY OF WASHINGTON COUNTY; 1901
Lamb, Wallace; LAKE GEORGE AND LAKE CHAMPLAIN VALLEYS
LAKE GEORGE MIRROR; sundry copies 1896 to 1918
Lossing, B.J.; THE HUDSON
Lonergan, C.; TICONDEROGA, HISTORIC PORTAGE
MaGuire, Robert; HISTORY OF FT. TICONDEROGA FERRY
NEW YORK STATE FOREST COMMISSION REPORT; 1891
NEW YORK STATE LEGISLATIVE REPORT ON LAKE GEORGE WATER
     CONDITIONS; 1945
Parkman, Francis; LAKE GEORGE AND LAKE CHAMPLAIN; 1885
Parkman, Francis; MONTCALM AND WOLF
Ringold, Don; HUDSON RIVER DAYLINE
Samson, W.H.; MOHICAN POINT
Seelye, Elizabeth; LAKE GEORGE IN HISTORY; 1896
Smith; HISTORY OF WARREN COUNTY; 1885
Stoddard, S.R.; THE ADIRONDACKS; 1873-1875
Stoddard, S.R.; LAKE GEORGE, A BOOK OF TODAY; 1873-1911
Ticonderoga Historical Society; TICONDEROGA, PATCHES AND PATTERNS
     FROM ITS PAST
Van DerWater, F.; LAKE GEORGE AND LAKE CHAMPLAIN
White, William Chapman; ADIRONDACK COUNTRY; 1954
Wolf, L.M.; SON OF THE WILDERNESS, JOHN MUIR

Sidelight from a D & M Steam Locomotive wrecked near Crown Point. Several years later a farmer plowed it up in his field.

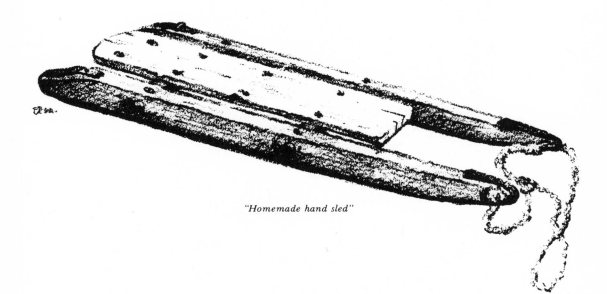

"Homemade hand sled"